# LAUNDRETTES AND LOVERS

# LAUNDRETTES AND LOVERS

## From Storyboard to Billboard

Twenty Years of a British Film Company

First published 2003 by Boxtree an imprint of Pan Macmillan Ltd
20 New Wharf Road London N1 9RR
Basingstoke and Oxford
Associated companies throughout the world
www.panmacmillan.com

ISBN 0 7522 6192 4

**Editors & Researchers for Working Title Films:** Juliette Dow, Amelia Granger, Deborah Harding
**US Researcher:** Christina de la Bédoyère
**Talent Liaison:** Vicki Williams – UK; Evan Hayes – US
**Editors for Pan Macmillan:** Emma Marriott; Natalie Jerome; Annie Schafheitle

**Photographers/Agencies**
*p10* Gaby Dellal © Gaby Dellal; *p14* Bertrand Rindoff © Bertrand Rindoff/Alpha Press; *p25* Anton Corbijn © Anton Corbijn; *p87* Nick Wall © Nick Wall *p106-107* Albert Watson © Albert Watson; *p114-115* Pamela Hanson © Pamela Hanson; *p234* Cathal MacIlwaine © Cathal MacIlwaine; *p19, 241, 244, 245, 255* Peter Mountain © Peter Mountain/Katz Pictures; *p151, 162, 196, 216, 224, 225, 228, 230, 234, 248, 250, 252,256-257* Greg Williams © Greg Williams; *p227* Dave Hogan © Getty Images; *p254* Lorenzo Agius © Lorenzo Agius

**Extracts**
*p30-33, 34* Extracted from 'Dreaming and Scheming' by Hanif Kureishi © Hanif Kureishi 2001. First published in the UK by Faber & Faber Ltd in 2002. Reproduced by permission of Rogers, Coleridge & White Ltd, 20 Powis Mews, London W11 1JN
*p76* Extract from 'Derek Jarman, A Biography' by Tony Peake © Little Brown and Co., A division of Time Warner Books UK. Reproduced by kind permission of Tony Peake. *p96* Extract from 'And the Winner Isn't' by Duncan Kenworthy for The Independent on Sunday, 26 March 1995. © Duncan Kenworthy 1995. Reproduced by kind permission of Duncan Kenworthy.

**Soundtrack Artwork**
*p217* From the Motion Picture *About a Boy*, Original Soundtrack composed and performed by Badly Drawn Boy: Album Sleeve Artwork © XL Recordings/Andy Votel 2002

9 8 7 6 5 4 3 2 1

A CIP catalogue record for this book is available from the British Library.

Designed by **BRILL**
Colour reproduction by Aylesbury Studios Bromley Ltd
Printed by Butler and Tanner Ltd, Frome, Somerset

**Thanks to:**
**For Working Title Films/Universal:** Tracie Amis, Nick Angel, Christina Angeloudes, Liza Chasin, Justine Concannon, Chloé Dorigan, Tim Easthill, Nicki Garrett, Shefali Ghosh, Debra Hayward, Alex Hill, Aliza James, Rachel Kennedy, David Livingstone, Kate Luczyc-Wyhowska, Gráinne McKenna, Callum Metcalfe, Angela Morrison, Luke Parker Bowles, Matt Plumb, Rachael Prior, Charlotte Saint, Sheeraz Shah, Lucy Wainwright, Natascha Wharton, Michelle Wright, Sarah-Jane Wright
**Additional Thanks to:** Cate Blanchett, Adam Brooks, Sam Cohn, Anton Corbijn, Richard Curtis, James Ellis, Tim Forrester, Jane Frazer, Jocelyn Fritz, Elaine Goldsmith Thomas, Claudia Gray, Duncan Kenworthy, Stephanie Langhoff, David Leland, Melissa Moseley, Peter Mountain, Tony Peake, Vanessa Pereira, Sarah Radclyffe, Tim Robbins, Gary Teetzel, Leah Thomas, Bart Walker, Peter Wickes and Greg Williams.
**For Comic Relief:** Kevin Cahill, Emma Freud

The Editors would like to thank Tim Bevan and Eric Fellner for their co-operation and commitment to the project.

Finally, a huge thank you to all the photographers, to all those who contributed text pieces and especially to everyone who has worked for Working Title Films over the years, in whatever capacity.

Really rather gorgeously, Working Title Films are donating their profits from this book to Comic Relief. So here is a quick word about what your purchase will help happen.

Comic Relief began on Christmas Day 1985 as a response to the terrible famine in Ethiopia. Richard Curtis, our co-founder, galvanized the comedy community into action and every penny of the money raised was used to help people in seriously difficult circumstances. Since then, people working in comedy have endlessly given us their cleverness and commitment – and as a result the public have given us an unbelievable £305 million. Because of the generosity of companies like Working Title who help us cover our costs, all – really all – of the money raised has been spent on projects supporting thousands and thousands of individuals in Africa and the UK. This means that some of the cash you spent on this book will go directly to change the life of someone having an unimaginably tough time.

In Africa, the money made from your buying this book will go to extraordinary projects making loans to widows of the Rwandan genocide to start their own businesses, or helping get orphaned street kids off the streets and into school and homes, or helping the children of women living with AIDS. In the UK it might help a girl forced into prostitution at twelve to rebuild her life, it might provide refuge for a woman who has had to leave home because her husband is beating her up, or it might help a homeless teenager whose life has nearly been destroyed by drug and alcohol problems, to get back to a home and a job.

Let me give you one example – Banele is a four-year-old from Johannesburg. His dad died two years ago. We met his mum last year when she was very sick with AIDS and two weeks later she died too. Banele has a brother and sister aged three and two – they have a home but literally nothing else, and no one else, in their lives. Now, however, they have just one glimmer of hope. Because of a Comic Relief grant the three children are going to nursery school for a few hours each day. There they get two square meals and there are grown-ups in their lives teaching and looking out for them. Banele is a kid full of life and energy but deep down he has all the problems of a child orphaned too young who is in charge of two tiny siblings. Comic Relief cash is making the difference between having a chance and having none at all.

Just buying this book will help to change the life of someone you will never meet – someone who will never have a chance to thank you. So, on their behalf – huge, great, enormous thanks.

And also, obviously, big thanks to Working Title, who have supported Comic Relief unquestioningly and wholeheartedly for the last decade. They've not only given us the money from movie premieres, but they've also provided funding for bread-and-butter stuff – like printing fundraising packs and donation envelopes which have helped raise hundreds and thousands of pounds for us to give away in the best way we can.

It is my passionate hope that they keep making movies for another twenty years and continue to spend some of their hard-earned cash, not to mention any ill-gotten gains, on us.

**KEVIN CAHILL**
Chief Executive, Comic Relief

# **INTRODUCTION** TIM BEVAN

In the mid-1980s, when I co-produced *My Beautiful Laundrette* and Eric produced *Sid and Nancy*, I doubt if either of us thought we would still be around in the film business in a year's time, let alone twenty. In an attempt to mark this time and as a tribute to all those who have built Working Title we decided to publish this book of images and anecdotes from two decades of our movies.

We both cut our teeth producing music videos in the early 1980s. Music videos had just taken off and were a brilliant forum for getting started in the film business. I first met Eric at this time – I remember visiting his office and seeing a lot of very stylish, very skinny and very hairy people around. With Eric, the style and skinniness remain but sadly not the hair. Through the eighties our careers ran in parallel and he was someone whom I always thought I would like to work with given the right moment.

Sarah Radclyffe and I started Working Title in 1984 from our music video business Aldabra. I had met Sarah when she was crewing one of Channel 4's first commissions – *The Comic Strip Presents…* I didn't get a job on the show but we started a company together – it was 1982. Somewhat idealistically we both had aspirations to produce movies – if you could make a video then why not a movie? Beyond this there really was no plan. We began to get movie people to make videos – Nic Roeg, Derek Jarman and Stephen Frears among others – and our first two Working Title film productions came from these relationships. Many of the attributes necessary for being a movie producer were unwittingly honed at this time. I rapidly learnt that one's own personality was the key and that it all hinged on getting on with the commissioner. In years to come, whether soliciting movie talent from Hollywood agents, persuading a director or writer to come on board a film project or raising the money for a movie, it has all required the same salesmanship, or as some would call it – brinkmanship.

The UK film landscape at the time was changing. There were two big companies: EMI and Goldcrest. There was a lot of fanfare about the latter, it being a collection of successful British talent joined together who were going to make big movies and take on Hollywood. At the same time there were smaller financing outfits starting up: British Screen, run by Simon Relph; Zenith, run by Charles Denton and Margaret Matheson; and most importantly Channel 4, the new television channel with a dedicated film wing run by David Rose and Karin Bamborough. It was these smaller outfits that were so supportive of the fledgling Working Title. The irony was that by the end of the 1980s the two big companies had disappeared, and the talent backed by the smaller outfits would form the backbone of British film for the next twenty years.

Stephen Frears had just made a movie called *The Hit* when we asked him to make a video for Heaven 17. I think he liked the energy and youth of the people he met on the video – Oliver Stapleton the DP, Hugo Wyhowski the designer and Jane Frazer the production manager, who until 2000 was Working Title's Head of Production. Over the years Stephen has made several films with Working Title; he has always loved working with young people with something to say.

Shortly after completing the video, the writer Hanif Kureishi posted the script of *My Beautiful Laundrette* through Stephen's letterbox. Hanif had developed the script with the new Film Four arm. Stephen read it and like all of us thought that the writing took us to a

*Opposite:* **Eric Fellner (left) and Tim Bevan**

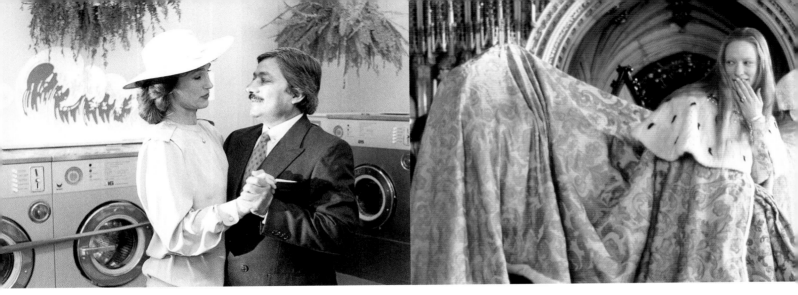

world that had not been seen before on film. Contemporary London seen through the eyes of a Pakistani and a gay one at that. Much to our surprise he gave Sarah and myself the script and asked us if we would produce it.

Stephen, Hanif and I went to see the Film Four executives. On the way in Stephen said to me, 'You know about film budgets don't you?' Not having a clue, I said, 'Of course.' And then, as we stepped into David Rose's office, he muttered, 'By the way I only make films in February' – it was November at the time.

When David and Karin asked when we would like to make the film I said 'February' and when they said how much I closed my eyes and said 'One million dollars'. Much to everyone's surprise, most of all mine, they said great! By February I had turned twenty-five. We all learnt as we went along. Stephen was very brave and accepted our motley crew of young, energetic, under-experienced people. Hanif introduced him to the world of Pakistani acting talent and somehow we muddled through. We, of course, all landed on our feet by casting Daniel Day-Lewis as one of the leads.

A number of times over the years, new stars have emerged through Working Title's films. If the film is good it is amazing the incremental excitement a rising star can create: Dan in the *Laundrette*, Emily Lloyd in *Wish You Were Here*, Hugh Grant in *Four Weddings and a Funeral*, Cate Blanchett in *Elizabeth*, Jamie Bell in *Billy Elliot*. All these films benefited hugely both commercially and critically from the bonus an audience feels in discovering new talent.

The *Laundrette* was originally intended as a television movie. It was only after the tremendous reception that it received at the Edinburgh Film Festival that we decided to take it out theatrically. This was a great bit of luck because on the back of the movie I really learnt how the movie business worked. I learnt that there were independent distributors in every country who would buy the distribution rights in the movie. I learnt that you could pre-sell those rights and make your film with that money. I learnt that there was a two-tier system in the film business – the Hollywood majors and the independents. I learnt that pretty much everything in the worldwide film business went back to one place, Hollywood.

Eric and I have been commuting to Hollywood several times a year for most of the last twenty years. Separately and then once we had joined forces, we both realized that if you

are going to work in the film business you have to have an ongoing and solid relationship with Los Angeles. All major decisions in film are made here regardless of where the film is being produced. Most film finance comes from Hollywood, most worldwide film distribution is based in Hollywood and most importantly it is where the main talent agencies are. Any director, writer, producer or actor from anywhere in the world who has had any success will be represented by one of the LA talent agencies. Without a relationship with the LA agents you will not go far.

Too many British producers see the American business as the enemy. Eric and I have worked with people in Hollywood right from the beginning and made good friends there. The assistants that we got to know in the 1980s, whether in the studios or the agencies, are now senior in their jobs and in some cases running their organizations. There is a way about Hollywood and the way that it does business, some would call it vulgarity, that I find exciting and stimulating. For the past twelve years we have had an office in LA run by Liza Chasin. She has grown up in the community there and is invaluable to our business in terms of contacts and maintaining a constant Hollywood presence.

After the *Laundrette* I was determined not to stand still. I had seen other producers falter while trying to put together a second movie. Sarah was invited by Derek Jarman to produce his *Caravaggio* for the BFI, and I was invited to produce *Personal Services*. We began to work with new talent: writers, directors, other people in the movie chain – and this has become 'the Working Title way', helping to keep the company on its toes creatively.

Using a combination of equity money from the UK, pre-sales to distribution companies and various tax schemes, we funded our movies through the rest of the 1980s. I realized that there was a lot to learn and that if you didn't know something then you asked someone who did. In this respect Working Title's external lawyer, Billy Hinshelwood played a very important role at this time, whilst on the funding side we were helped by another partner, Graham Bradstreet.

We put together a team of staff funded through our film fees, and as soon as the second and third movies got going we left the music video business behind. A few of the people who still work with the company today joined us at this time, notably Debra Hayward who, starting as Sarah's assistant, is now Head of Film in the UK, and an indispensable

**Tim Bevan and Eric Fellner receive the European Producers of the Year Award 1999 in Cannes** *Left to right:* **Eric Fellner, Alex Cox, Sarah Radclyffe, Gordon Warnecke, Shawn Slovo, Tim Bevan and Jodhi May**

member of the team. These were truly independent days – everybody worked hard and played hard. Most serious business was done in the pub after work, and for a while The George on Wardour Street became the centre of the British film business.

Every year we went to the Cannes Film Festival. I would cram in as many meetings as I could in a day, rushing up and down the Croisette, often bumping into Eric, equally frantic, coming the other way. Then, as a matter of course, you would stay up all night drinking at the Petit Carlton before starting again. The first Working Title film into competiton was *A World Apart*. In those days we would all cram into an apartment and queue for the bathroom to put on our tuxedos – a far cry from the luxury of the Hotel du Cap on recent visits… There is no doubt that if you are lucky enough to get a film into competition, standing on the red carpet and then watching the movie on the magnificent screen is heady stuff.

During this period we produced several movies, some good – *A World Apart*, *Wish You Were Here*, *Personal Services* – some bad, some indifferent and one career-changing – *The Tall Guy*. It was Anthony Jones, a London literary agent, who introduced me to Richard Curtis. Richard had had great success as a television comedy writer working closely with Rowan Atkinson and others on *Not the Nine O'Clock News* and *Blackadder*. *Camden Town Boy*, as it was then called, was Richard's first feature film script and Anthony introduced Richard to Working Title as worthy producers. In fact, *The Tall Guy* was not hugely successful as a movie, but it spawned great things. I had been able to put the financing of the film together using the benefit of a large television levy available in those days. A couple of years after the completion of the movie, despite it having under-performed, Working Title received a largish royalty cheque from the film's financier. This was totally unexpected and, for a struggling independent with no money, was heaven sent. Rather than banking it without a thought – which would have been my first instinct – I looked at who the profit participants in the film were and sent them each their share. Richard was so surprised that not only had he had fun making his movie but he was also seeing a royalty cheque from it (even though not that many people had been to see the film), that he rewarded this act of generosity by sending us his next screenplay, *Four Weddings and a Funeral*.

This was the beginning of one of the most successful relationships in recent British cinema history. From the outset Richard has been a great partner – he has always been the best company and his films fun to work on. He has also taught me the greatest lesson in film – that of keeping the quality control of a project sharply in focus right until the end of the creative process. Richard has been involved in every stage of all the films that he has worked on with us. As writer of the script he is guardian of the text, but as executive producer on *The Tall Guy*, *Four Weddings and a Funeral* and *Notting Hill*, director on *Love Actually* and co-writer and executive producer on *Bean* and *Bridget Jones's Diary*, he has also worked on the casting, crewing, editing and marketing of the films. Collectively (not including *Love Actually*) these titles have grossed over a billion dollars at the worldwide box office.

Sadly, the independent film business of the 1980s was not something that could last. Our ambitions were growing, films like *Map of the Human Heart* were pushing us to the limit, and without proper backing the business was not sustainable. We were spending too much time on trying to keep the whole thing afloat and not nearly enough on the really important thing – the content of the films. Working Title did not have a proper infrastructure and when our accountant was beginning each day with a can of Special Brew I knew that things had to change… I had met Michael Kuhn in the music video days. He and his colleague David Hockman had been the video commissioners for Polydor. I remembered them as two fat guys who used to take the mickey and never give us a job. In the early 1990s Michael had become more senior within PolyGram and was looking to diversify the company into film. On a trip to LA we got talking, and over the course of the next weeks and months he told me of his plans and I told him of our woes as an under-capitalized independent in the movie business. It seemed we each had what the other needed: for Michael the chance to get involved in a film production company, and for us a white knight.

PolyGram invested in the company and then acquired it, and by 1992 Working Title had evolved structure-wise into the sort of company that it is today. Sarah decided that she wanted to remain an independent producer and left to form her own company, and Eric joined as co-chairman. This was the start of a completely new Working Title and the beginning of a unique working partnership, which has turned the company into what it is today. Although complementary in our knowledge of the film business and our ambition, we are different as people – Eric more hesitant, whereas I am impulsive; he is a better 'people person' and I am a big reader. These many differences have somehow meshed to work brilliantly in what we do. I think this is principally because of a mutual respect whereby we know when not to tread on each other's toes.

The new Working Title was to be part of the PolyGram film strategy. We would be a production label, autonomous in terms of deciding the films that we would make, but tied in to PolyGram for distribution and finance – the spirit of independence with the resources of a studio. For Eric and myself, joint decision makers in matters of structure, business and creative direction, this was a golden opportunity. Our strategy was to oversee our films from the first kernel of an idea through to managing and participating in the decisions relating to their marketing and distribution. We wanted the process of getting a film to an audience to begin right at the start. This is not to say we would restrict ourselves to making commercial films only, but more that a million-dollar film needs to find a million-dollar audience and a seventy-million-dollar movie a seventy-million-dollar audience. We realized that any film, because of the capital cost, must have international appeal.

Our internal infrastructure consisted of a development department run by Liza in LA and Debra in London, a business affairs department that would make and paper all deals from a rights agreement through to a major star's contract run by our COO Angela Morrison (now four lawyers strong), and a physical production department liaising and monitoring all stages of each film's production, run by Jane Frazer initially and now by Michelle Wright. Eric and I also decided that although we would share in all major decisions – which films, what budget, director, cast etc. – we would split the films and run them individually, thus ensuring third parties could not divide and rule and we in turn could cover more ground.

The job of the production company is one of creation – enabling a film to come to life. This largely depends on who else is involved and where the idea originally came from. It can be a third-party creative relationship where Working Title provides finance, production structure, marketing and distribution oversight and some creative opinion – the films of the Coen Brothers, with whom we have made a number of pictures, would fall into this category. Another route is developing a book (*Bridget Jones's Diary*) or an idea from scratch (*Elizabeth*) and resultantly having a total hands-on creative involvement in all stages of the filmmaking: development, choice of writer, director, cast, crew, locations, style, shooting, editing, marketing and distribution.

We did not realize the true value of being part of a unified international distribution structure until we had our first major hit in 1994 with *Four Weddings and a Funeral*. One of Working Title's great pieces of luck is that the company was nearly ten years old and we had at least twenty films under our belt before the big one came (the second piece of good fortune was that we had managed to stay afloat until this point). For us the reality has always been making films that we have a passion for and enjoying the process – not the accolade of a hit. It meant that when the hit finally came we were more able to take it, and the following hits, in our stride.

*Four Weddings and a Funeral* was a blessed movie. The combination of Mike Newell, Duncan Kenworthy and Richard Curtis at the film's creative helm was a strong one. Richard's script was and is one of the best pieces of original film writing in many a long year. The casting was spot-on, the timing perfect – the world was down and needed cheering up. Just as importantly, PolyGram needed a hit and spent big monies promoting the film in the US, UK and France in particular. Michael Kuhn and Stewart Till pushed their international distribution machine to the maximum and reaped the rewards – a $250 million worldwide gross on a film that had cost under $5 million to make!

*Four Weddings* was inevitably a hard act to follow. We had met Rowan Atkinson on *The Tall Guy*. He was and is one of England's best-loved comedians, with his *Blackadder* and *Mr Bean* television shows being cult comedy classics. The idea of the *Bean* movie had been around for some time but our involvement meant we could hone it down and get the structure right. Like Richard, Rowan is a great perfectionist, involved at all stages of the filmmaking process on his movies – with *Bean* this paid off with another big worldwide hit. These two films were the beginning of an excellent run for Working Title through the 1990s. By working in America with the Coen brothers on *The Hudsucker Proxy*, *Fargo*, and *The Big Lebowski* and with Tim Robbins on *Bob Roberts* and *Dead Man Walking*, and in Europe with Larry Kasdan on *French Kiss*, Rowan Atkinson on *Bean*, and Richard Curtis on *Notting Hill*, we were able to combine quality with commercial success. Our films were European in feel wherever they were made, performing very well at the European box office thanks to the driving force of the PolyGram machine. This level of success enabled us to take some bigger risks on home-developed material.

*Elizabeth* was a classic Working Title production. Standing around in the corridor one day we internally decided that we would like to make a period movie, not in the tradition of British 'frock flicks' but something altogether grittier. We decided that Elizabeth's reign had great elements of the thriller about it. We screened my favourite film *The Godfather* to look at its structure. We threw the idea out to various writers – Michael Hirst, an old friend, came up with a great take and wrote a cracking first draft.

We did not want to fall into the British 'period film' groove so when looking for directors we made a list of non-obvious choices. Shekhar Kapur's *Bandit Queen* had impressed us all. He knew nothing about English history – brilliant – his journey of discovery would be the film's journey. We could not find our Elizabeth, the big names turned it down and the right actress seemed to be eluding us. Then we met Cate Blanchett and our prayers seemed to have been answered. As she was then unknown we had to screen test her – she shone, and the rest is history.

**Tim Bevan and Cate Blanchett between takes on the set of *Elizabeth***

All the people who worked on the movie were dedicated to Shekhar's vision. Thanks to the success of some of our other films we were able to push the budget and put the money into the sets and wardrobe that gave the film a larger feel. The completed film was seen and admired all around the world, got seven Oscar® nominations and won one, along with a handful of BAFTA wins. It was a blast.

At the end of the 1990s the entire PolyGram group was sold to Seagrams. Seagrams were only interested in the music assets, and with no buyer forthcoming for its film assets, Universal (also part of the Seagram group), subsequently took over the film assets of which Working Title was a part. Eric and I needed to ensure that we controlled our future. We decided that the most important thing was to retain creative autonomy while being part of a worldwide distribution structure. We wanted control to make the films that we wanted to as well as being able to continue developing new talent. In order to preserve this we structured an arrangement with Universal whereby a European financing partner, Canal Plus shared in the financing of the Working Title slate. The deal was to be run by Universal. Eric and I were a little apprehensive of dealing with studio executives but happily the relationship has been excellent. Stacey Snider, Ron Meyer and the team at Universal have been totally supportive. They inherited *Notting Hill* from PolyGram so our relationship started with a $350 million hit. They liked that. The studio business is a hit-driven business and Eric and I realized that in order to preserve our autonomy and to be able to make the smaller movies some of them needed to make good money.

So, in the space of the last few years, Working Title has hit its third decade and third phase – Hollywood producer. Unlike other Hollywood producers we live in London and make a vast range of films both in origin and scale; however, unlike any other British producers, our larger movies constantly make up part of a major studio's slate.

Being able to carry our slate from PolyGram to Universal enabled us to put films into production quickly: *Bridget Jones's Diary* and *Captain Corelli's Mandolin* were both manuscripts that we had acquired some years previously and in both cases the adaptations took a long time. Both proved labours of love to bring to the screen – *Bridget* was Eric's film, and *Corelli* mine. We experienced major ups and downs, script problems, production problems, deal problems – one was a major hit and one way more modest. However, I think that they did give us the confidence to make bigger movies with greater production values. Most importantly they were larger scale European content movies made within the Hollywood system.

By virtue of the fact that the same team has worked together for a long time, our development slate of potential movie projects was and is deep. It takes a long time to develop a project from idea to screen. The quickest we achieved was inside one year with *French Kiss*, though it normally takes on average two to five years. Our slate broadly falls into three areas – long-term creative partnerships: the Coens, Richard Curtis, Rowan Atkinson, Stephen Daldry; material that we buy as a book or screenplay – *Bridget Jones's Diary*, *Captain Corelli's Mandolin*; or original ideas or scripts – *Elizabeth*, *French Kiss*. At any given time across the Working Title and WT² slates there are probably fifty projects in development.

In the late 1990s we decided that as the company was getting bigger we would start a new label for smaller films. WT², run by Natascha Wharton, specifically designed to make first films by first-time directors, writers and other creative talent. WT²'s first production was *Billy Elliot*. Eric had followed the career of Stephen Daldry in the theatre and we offered him a deal to develop a film career. We all loved the screenplay and on the basis of this alone we greenlit the film. It was a perfect vehicle for the 'getting back to roots' purpose of WT² but it needed specific help at the marketing stage. Out of the demise of PolyGram we were able to keep two very important people: David Livingstone and Kate Luczyc-Wyhowska, who oversee the worldwide marketing and publicity on our films. Working closely on projects right from the script stage through to the billboard, David designs marketing strategies to make sure a film finds its audience. Without the worldwide distribution backing and a fantastic campaign *Billy Elliot* would have found an audience but at nothing like the level that it did.

With *About a Boy*, *Johnny English* and *Love Actually* recently released, *Thunderbirds* and *Wimbledon* in post-production and a sequel to *Bridget Jones's Diary* in production, we have been able to keep the ideal alive of making larger films here for a worldwide audience. In *Bridget*, *Johnny English* and *Thunderbirds* we have projects of a franchise-able nature. They serve as the commercial backbone to our business, enabling us to take risks on smaller films through WT² or through our new Australian outpost – *Ned Kelly* being the first of these – or indeed to make the larger quality films such as the Coens' *O Brother, Where Art Thou?* or *The Man Who Wasn't There*.

There have been lots of films – Eric and I have produced seventy-one so far between us – millions of images, many diverse personalities and stories – some of which are recounted in the following pages. Writing this there does seem to have been a strange logic to the evolution; we have worked with many great people at all stages of the process and been lucky enough ourselves to learn along the way. Ultimately the films must speak for themselves, and in their own way I am proud of them all.

**Aurelia (Lucia Moniz) chases a paper trail in *Love Actually***

# 1980s

### THE EARLY YEARS

MY BEAUTIFUL LAUNDRETTE
WISH YOU WERE HERE
PERSONAL SERVICES
SAMMY AND ROSIE GET LAID
A WORLD APART
THE TALL GUY

**Producer Sarah Radclyffe on the set of *A World Apart***

**Lena (Tilda Swinton) poses for the artist in Derek Jarman's *Caravaggio***

## SARAH RADCLYFFE
### Co-Founder, Working Title Films

One thing stands out resoundingly, and that's how incredibly lucky Tim and I were. *My Beautiful Laundrette* – not a first draft but an incredibly fresh, clever, funny, fully developed screenplay, with an extremely talented director attached – landed in our laps, and the finance (just one source – Channel 4) followed almost immediately.

Previously Tim and I had been making music videos – a calculated decision to enable us to get to meet and work with directors whose work we admired. With absolutely no track record at all, it wasn't exactly possible to ring up A-list directors and say we'd like to produce their next film. We could, however, due to the novelty value at the time, persuade them to direct a music video. We made over a hundred (certainly none of them award-winning!).

I am often told that making films is a bit like having children – nature somehow manages to completely wipe the pain from one's memory. Not quite true, as I can certainly vividly remember sobbing pathetically on Caroline Hewitt's shoulder whilst in Zimbabwe on *A World Apart*. However my memories of *My Beautiful Laundrette*, Working Title's first venture into production, seem to concur with everyone else's: it was fun – great fun – and exciting and the work of a very closely knit team, led with both energy and humour by Stephen Frears who we all learnt so much from. It was also actually the only film that Tim and I really produced together. Possibly due to the fact it was the only project we both felt equally passionate about, we then quickly moved into what was, for me, the perfect partnership. I was allowed to make the films that I wanted to, he made the films that he wanted to, and even better, as far as I was concerned, was that he was prepared to take the overall responsibility of getting the finance in place.

After *My Beautiful Laundrette*, I reunited with Derek Jarman on *Caravaggio*. Actually Derek should really be held responsible for initiating Working Title as after I produced *The Tempest* for him, he asked us to do our first music video. Whether on music videos or feature films, working with Derek was a complete joy. His qualities of leadership and his ability to make absolutely everybody, including the trainees, feel important and part of his extended family were something that I was always very conscious of trying to bring back from the set into the office – I was always an advocate of an open-plan environment with as little as possible going on behind closed doors. Looking back, I think Tim was probably amazingly tolerant of my somewhat 'hippyish' work ethic.

*Caravaggio* was followed by David Leland's *Wish You Were Here* and it was while I was 'safely' ensconced down in Bournemouth that Tim quite rightly decided that it was time we had some help on the financial side, and Graham Bradstreet was brought into the mix.

The most heart-stopping moment of *Wish You Were Here* was arriving back at the hotel at the end of a day, to find the entire (or what seemed at the time to be the entire) South-eastern police force awaiting my return. Luckily a case of mistaken identity. The white powder that they gleefully told me they had found in one of my crew's bedrooms turned out to be nothing more than plant food.

Back in London, I remember enjoying one of those rare periods in my career in the film industry when I could actually concentrate on what I really, really wanted to do, which was to work with Shawn Slovo on *A World Apart*, certainly by far the best script I had ever read, with all the ingredients I was looking for – a wonderfully engaging personal story which also had a lot to say to the whole world. Tim and Graham took on the business of putting the finance together. Ignorance is, of course, bliss – had I known at the time that not only would the money go into the bank account in a suitcase, but that it would also unfortunately go out the same day in the same suitcase, I might not have left on the plane for Zimbabwe quite so full of adrenalin and excitement.

Filming *A World Apart* was incredibly hard. The money did fall apart – more than once. The complexity of filming in Bulawayo when all previous films made in Zimbabwe had been made up in Harare, combined with the naivety with which we set out, proved almost too hard.

Here I have to mention the wonderful Clarissa Troop without whom it probably could never have been finished. We had run out of money yet again, we had reached the limit on my, and most of my production team's, credit cards, and we needed to call back at least one hundred of the extras from the previous day. There was literally no money to pay them. We hadn't finished the sequence – we needed those shots. At that moment Clarissa, our assistant accountant, admitted to having kept back about $10 each week out of the petty cash, at the very, very, very back of the safe in case of 'a rainy day'. The accumulated amount, needless to say, did save the day. Tough, but also incredibly rewarding. Watching the film come together safely back in London not only rapidly dispelled images of car bombs, having to eat kudu's liver with a group of prospective financiers and the inevitable unpaid bills, but also justified the hard work we all put in. Making it may have been hard, I'm sure the constant re-financing was equally torturous. I am sure I speak for all of us when I say that walking down the carpet to receive awards for *A World Apart* really was a dream come true and also an extremely hard act to follow.

**Sarah Radclyffe stands on the Bulawayo railway tracks on location for *A World Apart***

## NICOLAS ROEG
Director

Well, well, well – I was right. When I shut the door on tall, handsome Tim after he had come round to my flat to talk about making an extended promo for a Roger Waters Pink Floyd album, I thought 'That's a major film producer bursting out of the seams of video promos'. In fact, the next time he came round, rather to his amazement, I sent him off with about three books I wanted to make into films, including Barbara Tuchman's *A Distant Mirror*.

On reflection I am sure, at the time, Tim was rather bemused by it all. We made the promo. It was a wild and wonderful affair. We shot just outside Seattle and it had one of the most terrifying, daring and exciting images of a beautiful naked girl with her arms wide apart standing up on the back footrests behind the driver of a huge motorcycle as it sped away from the camera – and then towards it – down a fifty-mile dead-straight Washington State highway.

I like to think that shoot was an important moment for Tim in a life decision to push on to bigger and more dangerous ventures. Who knows? But the 'time train' rushed on, and out of Aldabra grew Working Title. Tim, Eric and the company have attracted a wonderful bunch of movie talent in front of and behind the camera and they have made an astounding collection of films. I knew it would happen the moment I shut the door behind Tim.

## KARIN BAMBOROUGH
Deputy Head Single Film and Drama, Channel 4, 1981–90

In the early summer of 1984, when I was an assistant commissioning editor at Channel 4, I invited a young writer called Hanif Kureishi to lunch. I'd liked and admired his work in the theatre, and wondered if he might be interested in writing for film. He was, and he told me a story over lunch, on the basis of which, with David Rose's blessing, I commissioned him to write a screenplay. In those days it was that simple. The screenplay he delivered had no connection whatsoever with the story I'd commissioned, but what the hell. It was vibrant, provocative, funny and unexpected. That was the genesis of *My Beautiful Laundrette*.

Before we'd even begun to think about directors, Hanif very smartly posted the script through Stephen Frears' letterbox. And Stephen equally smartly brought in Tim and Sarah as producers. So we had the script and the team; the only thing we didn't have was the money, we were already fully committed for that financial year. And we didn't think there was much chance of raising commercial finance for a film about a gay Pakistani laundrette owner in Peckham.

Tim and Sarah knew *Laundrette* was our first reserve if funds came free, but they didn't hang around waiting for the green light, they got on with it. So, when a month or so later another film did collapse, they had everything lined up and were ready to go. They had the tightest of budgets and schedules, but they were determined to make it work, and they did. You would never have guessed that they hadn't made a feature film before.

*Left to right:* **The Little Russell Street office: Sophie Franks, Jane Frazer, Elizabeth Trafford, Sarah Radclyffe, Tim Bevan, Volker Stoxx and Luc Roeg**

My first brush with Working Title was just after they had made *My Beautiful Laundrette*, and I was employed to run the Aldabra office. Working Title was in Little Russell Street and Aldabra just across the road on New Oxford Street. It was an eccentric pair of offices to say the least. There were invariably phones being chucked around in frustration at projects taking longer to get off the ground than was appreciated and the inevitable 'necessary' visits across the road from all the girls in the Aldabra office when Daniel Day-Lewis was around. Ultimately we all moved to Livonia Street, where I believe our behaviour became a lot more grown-up.
– **Clarissa Troop, Aldabra/Working Title Films**

I first met Tim on the set of a Spear Of Destiny video in 1983. I was working as an assistant director for Aldabra. The video was being directed by Volker Stoxx, who was more glamorous and highly strung than any of the rock bands he worked for! It was the beginning of a very happy and somewhat mad period of my career and life. Tim and Sarah asked me to join Aldabra as a producer, an offer too good to refuse. It was a boom time in music videos which created a lot of exciting opportunities for a young generation of filmmakers and thanks to Tim and Sarah I jumped in head first. It was a chance to experiment with film and, more importantly, to convince the record companies to let us go to exotic locations.
– **Luc Roeg, Producer**

It was the early days for me when, as assistant to Debbie McWilliams, I was involved in the casting process of *My Beautiful Laundrette*. I have a lasting memory of the bleached blond Daniel Day-Lewis visiting our office, presenting us with a bottle of Polish spirits then whizzing round and round on my chair, eventually breaking it and, only just, avoiding being spun out of the third-floor window!
**– Michelle Guish,
Casting Director**

**The kiss: Johnny (Daniel Day-Lewis, left) and Omar (Gordon Warnecke) in *My Beautiful Laundrette***
Gordon and myself eye each other warily, chewing extra strong mints and chatting about our girlfriends. The clock's ticking. Stephen saunters in, plimsolls squeaking on lino. 'I'm just going down to the shops for a Mars bar, when I get back tell me where to put the camera.' Our eyes flash: one anxiety eclipsed by another. We're about to direct our first scene in a movie. Snogging's a doddle. Thanks Stephen. Bastard.
**– Daniel Day-Lewis, Actor**

In preparation for the kissing scenes, I imagined Daniel was Sigourney Weaver. The excellent writing made sense of the fact that we had to kiss so we just got on and did it. Daniel was always professional in his approach and that made doing these scenes a lot easier.
**– Gordon Warnecke, Actor**

# MARGARET MATHESON
Producer

I first met Sarah Radclyffe in the lunch queue at Cranks, introduced by the director Marek Kanievska. Marek and I were working on *Muck and Brass*, a television series starring Mel Smith in his first straight role. Sarah and Marek had met a while back working in a ski shop. She was producing six *Comic Strip* films and I think Tim Bevan came in for a job on one of them, but didn't get it. The upshot of this encounter was that they started Aldabra, making music videos but they wanted to produce feature films so they hired Luc Roeg to run Aldabra and formed Working Title.

At about the same time Charles Denton and I had started Zenith, a production company wholly owned by Central Independent Television. Having a monopoly and famously 'a licence to print money', ITV companies were at the time subject to the ITV Levy, a tax on advertising income. Zenith was producing and part-financing both features and television. Through structuring our deals to maximize income from overseas sales, which were not subject to the Levy, we were able to finance films on a tax-efficient basis. When Working Title burst onto the scene with *My Beautiful Laundrette*, we were natural collaborators. We had money. They were terrific producers. *The Hit*, the first feature developed by Zenith, was directed by Stephen Frears. He went on to direct *My Beautiful Laundrette,* which I first saw at a screening for Denis O'Brien, the big cheese at HandMade Films, who walked out halfway through.

Meanwhile, Zenith was working with Eric Fellner, who had produced a concert film and a documentary about Duran Duran, through his company Initial, after which he came back to us with a screenplay by Alex Cox and Abbe Wool called *Love Kills* – a love story about Sid Vicious and Nancy Spungen. This was Eric's first feature, *Sid and Nancy*, directed by Alex Cox. Zenith was also involved with *Personal Services*, *Wish You Were Here* and *For Queen and Country* – five or so very enjoyable years.

# SIMON RELPH
Producer

Sometime in late 1983 or early 1984 I received a call from my friend, and as it happened recently joined partner in Greenpoint films, Stephen Frears. He was getting involved in an extremely low-budget TV feature film for Channel 4 written by Hanif Kureishi, much too small, he said, for Greenpoint. It was going to be produced by these two very clever young people Sarah Radclyffe and Tim Bevan who were setting up a new company to do it. I knew Sarah a bit because she had worked with my father at Don Boyd's company but I didn't know Tim at all. Stephen told me that Tim hadn't made a feature before and asked me if I would mind meeting up with him to pass on a few tricks of the trade. Tim invited me round to Aldabra's office, where, over sandwiches, he bombarded me with questions, most of which I think I was able to answer, although at that time I had only produced three pictures myself. I think we did that on a couple of occasions and the rest is history.

**Nancy Spungen (Chloe Webb) and Sid Vicious (Gary Oldman) in Alex Cox's *Sid and Nancy***

**Christine Painter (Julie Walters) nervously awaits the arrival of the police in *Personal Services***

On *Personal Services* I represented director Terry Jones, writer David Leland and even Streatham's own infamous madame herself, Cynthia Payne. Preparations for this movie were hilarious – prison visits to Madame Cyn, sex parties at Ambleside Avenue and more I cannot mention.
– **Jenne Casarotto, Agent**

**Omar (Gordon Warnecke, left)
and Johnny (Daniel Day Lewis)
in the Laundrette**
Daniel went to watch Millwall
Football Club to get into character
before filming. Because I am a mad
Arsenal supporter, this was the only
part of his character development
he got wrong.
**– Gordon Warnecke, Actor**

While I was Head of Drama in Channel 4's early days and running Film on Four in the eighties, people were always asking what it was we were looking for in the films we commissioned. It was a tough question. We were committed to bringing new talent and fresh voices to the screen. I thought it was our job to avoid the fashionable or the obviously derivative. We wanted to support original writing and directors with a fresh outlook. But I didn't feel it was our job to be prescriptive about Film on Four. Once Working Title had produced a number of features for the channel, their distinctive body of work provided one answer to that question.
**– David Rose, Head of Drama, Channel 4 1981-90**

# HANIF KUREISHI
*Writer, My Beautiful Laundrette*

### Introduction to *My Beautiful Laundrette*

I think I may have been one of the first film editors to work for Working Title when Tim, Sarah and Jane asked me to come over and discuss the forthcoming production of *My Beautiful Laundrette*. They sat me down in those little upstairs offices in Little Russell Street, and said, well, we have never really made a film quite like this before and we know absolutely nothing about your side of it, so if you wouldn't mind telling us what to expect, that's what we will do. So, I explained the whole deal from the first day of shoot in the cutting room, right up to the finished print and that's what we did and it went like a dream. This immediately disproved Hanif's jokey tag for the company, 'Not Working Title'.
**– Mick Audsley, Editor**

**Oliver Stapleton (centre) with Daniel Day-Lewis (right) in the Laundrette**
During production I became ill with Hepatitis A, which I caught whilst shooting the Rolling Stones in Brazil. After one day in bed, a car picked me up and I went back to work in a wheelchair covered in a large blanket. This scarf may have been a few weeks later!
**– Oliver Stapleton, Cinematographer**

I wrote the script of *My Beautiful Laundrette* in my uncle's house in Karachi, Pakistan, in February 1984, during the night. As I wrote, cocks crowed and the call to prayer reverberated through crackly speakers from a nearby mosque. It was impossible to sleep. One morning as I sat on the verandah having breakfast, I had a phone call from Howard Davies, a director with the Royal Shakespeare Company, with whom I'd worked twice before. He wanted to direct Brecht's *Mother Courage*, with Judi Dench in the lead role. He wanted me to adapt it.

That summer, back in England and Howard's place in Stratford-upon-Avon, I sat in the orchard with two pads of paper in front of me: on one I rewrote *My Beautiful Laundrette* and on the other I adapted Brecht from a literal translation into language that could be spoken by RSC actors.

As *Laundrette* was the first film I'd written, and I was primarily a playwright, I wrote each scene of the film like a little scene for a play, with the action written like stage directions and with lots of dialogue. Then I'd cut most of the dialogue and add more stage directions, often set in cars, or with people running about, to keep the thing moving, since films required action.

I'd had a couple of lunches with Karin Bamborough of Channel 4. She wanted me to write something for Film on Four. I was extremely keen. For me Film on Four had taken over from the BBC's *Play for Today* in presenting serious contemporary drama on TV to a wide audience. The work of TV writers like Alan Bennett (much of it directed by Stephen Frears), Dennis Potter, Harold Pinter, Alan Plater and David Mercer influenced me greatly when I was young and living at home in the suburbs. On my way up to London the morning after a *Play for Today* I'd sit in the train listening to people discussing the previous night's drama and interrupt them with my own opinions.

The great advantage of TV drama was the people who watched it; difficult, challenging things could be said about contemporary life. The theatre, despite efforts of touring companies and so on, had failed to get its ideas beyond a small enthusiastic audience.

When I finished a draft of *My Beautiful Laundrette*, and *Mother Courage* had gone into rehearsal, Karin Bamborough, David Rose and I discussed directors for the film.

A couple of days later I went to see a friend, David Gothard, who was then running Riverside Studios. I often went for a walk by the river in the early evening, and then I'd sit in David's office. He always had the new books and latest magazines; and whoever was appearing at Riverside would be around. Riverside stood for tolerance, scepticism and intelligence. The feeling there was that works of art, plays, books and so on, were important. This is a rare thing in England. For many writers, actors, dancers and artists, Riverside was what a university should be: a place to learn and talk and work and meet your contemporaries. There was no other place like it in London and David Gothard was the great encourager, getting work on and introducing people to one another.

**Shooting outside the Laundrette with car**

*My Beautiful Laundrette* was the first 'successful' film I shot, as well as being the first of eight films I made with Stephen Frears. The colours of the film reflected a slow transition for me from the world of pop videos to the world of feature film.
**– Oliver Stapleton, Cinematographer**

He suggested I ask Stephen Frears to direct the film. I thought this an excellent idea, except that I admired Frears too much to have the nerve to ring him. David Gothard did this and I cycled to Stephen's house in Notting Hill, where he lived in a street known as 'director's row' because of the number of film directors living there.

He said he wanted to shoot my film in February. As it was November already I pointed out that February might be a little soon. Would there be time to prepare, to rewrite? But he had a theory: when you have a problem, he said, bring things forward; do them sooner rather than later. And anyway, February was a good month for him; he made his best films then; England looked especially unpleasant; and people worked faster in the cold. The producers, Tim Bevan and Sarah Radclyffe, Stephen had worked with before, on promos for rock bands. So the film was set up and I started to rewrite. Stephen and I had long talks, each of us pacing up and down the same piece of carpet, in different directions.

The film started off as an epic. It was to be like *The Godfather*, opening in the past with the arrival of an immigrant family in England and showing their progress to the present. There were to be many scenes set in the 1950s; people would eat bread and dripping and get off boats a lot; there would be scenes of Johnny and Omar as children and large-scale set pieces of racist marches with scenes of mass violence.

We soon decided it was impossible to make a film of such scale. That film is still to be made. Instead I set the film in the present, though references to the past remain.

It was shot in six weeks in February and March 1985 on a low budget and 16mm film. For this I was glad. There were no commercial pressures on us, no one had a lot of money invested in the film who would tell us what to do. And I was tired of seeing lavish films set in exotic locations; it seemed to me that anyone could make such films, providing they had an old book, a hot country, new technology and were capable of aiming the camera at an attractive landscape in the hot country in front of which stood a star in a perfectly clean costume delivering lines from the old book.

We decided the film was to have gangsters and thriller elements, since the gangster film is the form that corresponds most closely to the city, with its gangs and violence. And the film was to be an amusement, despite its references to racism, unemployment and Thatcherism. Irony is the modern mode, a way of commenting on bleakness and cruelty without falling into dourness and didacticism. And ever since the first time I heard people in a theatre laugh during a play of mine, I've wanted it to happen again and again.

We found actors – Saeed Jaffrey, for whom I'd written the part; and Roshan Seth I'd seen in David Hare's play *Map of the World*, commanding that huge stage at the National with complete authority. I skidded through the snow to see Shirley Anne Field and on arriving at her flat was so delighted by her charm and enthusiasm, and so ashamed of the smallness of her part, that there and then I added the material about the magic potions, the moving furniture and the walking trousers. It must have seemed that the rest of the film was peripheral and she would be playing the lead in a kind of *Exorcist* movie with a gay Pakistani, a drug-dealer and a fluff-drying spin-drier in the background.

Soon we stood under railway bridges in Vauxhall at two in the morning in March; we knocked the back wall out of someone's flat and erected a platform outside to serve as the balcony of Papa's flat, which had so many railway lines dipping and criss-crossing beside and above it that inside you shook like peas in maracas; in an old shop we built a laundrette of such authenticity that people came in off the street with their washing; and I stood on the set making up dialogue before the actors did it themselves, and added one or two new scenes.

When shooting was finished and we had about two-and-a-quarter hours of material strung together, we decided to have a showing for a group of 'wise ones'. They would be film directors, novelists and film writers who'd give us their opinions and thereby aid in editing the film. So I sat at the back of the small viewing cinema as they watched the film. We then cut forty-five minutes out.

The film played at the Edinburgh Film Festival and then went into the cinema.

## STEPHEN FREARS
*Director, My Beautiful Laundrette*

### About the *Laundrette*

Whatever Frears wears, he always
looks as if he's slept in his clothes and
his hair just stands straight up on top
and shoots out at the sides as if he's
been electrocuted. His idea of
dressing up is to put on a clean pair
of plimsolls. The sartorial message is:
I can't think about all that stuff, it
means nothing to me, I'm a bohemian
not a fashion slave. When we were
shooting the *Laundrette,* Daniel Day-
Lewis would go up to Stephen as if
Stephen were a tramp, and press 20p
in his hand, saying: 'Please accept this
on behalf of the Salvation Army and
buy yourself a cup of tea!'.
**– Hanif Kureishi, Writer**

I'm trying to remember but it's all a long time ago. In 1985, after *The Hit* was released, I was
asked to make a music video by a group called, I think, Heaven 17. I hadn't a clue how you
made them but my agent said she knew this young producer who had looked after Nic
Roeg in a similar situation. That was Tim Bevan.

He worked with his partner Sarah Radclyffe in a single largish room in Little Russell Street
and they made, I suppose, music videos though Sarah seemed to have produced Derek
Jarman's films. It was all a new world to me. I can't believe the video was any good but at
the end most of the young crew asked me to sign their application forms for the ACTT
(Association of Cinematographic Television Technicians). At the time – younger readers will
need to know – you had to belong to a trade union to work in the film industry. Can there
really have been such a time? Mrs Thatcher soon ended all that.

I had probably just been handed the script of *My Beautiful Laundrette*. I belonged to a company of competitive contemporaries and friends with whom I was already having rows and – such was the idiotic competitiveness – was mainly concerned that this script shouldn't fall into their hands. So I said to Tim in my best Lindsay Anderson-ish manner: 'Here. You'd better produce this', and gave him the script.

Gods knows what he thought. I doubt if gay Pakistani laundrette-owners were high on the list of fashionable subjects with which an ambitious young producer would advance his career. Two days later we went to Channel 4 to tell them that I wanted to make the film – only immediately. Tim laid out a plan of how to make it. Channel 4 had a bad reputation for taking ages to reach a decision but at 5.00p.m. on the same day David Rose rang and I knew the film was going to be made. That's how it seemed to me, anyway. Twenty years later Karin Bamborough, who shared the cupboard out of which Channel 4 films were made, told me that another film had just collapsed and there were we to fill the gap. Two months later we were filming.

A future friend said that, when she saw *My Beautiful Laundrette*, she assumed it was made by a man of twenty-four who wore leather trousers. At the time I was forty-four and had three children. But, of course, it was the new generation who made the difference. Hanif Kureishi, whose first film it was; Oliver Stapleton, ditto (well, there had been something in Scotland with Bryan Forbes); Hugo Luczyc-Wyhowski with whom I did three more films; Dan Day-Lewis, of course; and Tim, the child producer. Simon Relph, one of the friends I was busy fighting, said Tim was on the phone the whole time asking him what to do although I'd sneered that Simon wouldn't know how to make a film this cheap. Jane Frazer, the production manager, said she went home and cried every night. The experienced first assistant, Simon Hinckley, was telling them what had to be done.

But the film was made in six weeks, was good fun, and when Jeremy Isaacs put his thumb up while he was watching the first cut, I figured we'd made a good TV programme.

It was as if Christmas had come. At the first showing, at BAFTA, I shouted at Derek Malcolm that this was television and he shouldn't be there. He subsequently wrote the review that convinced Romaine Hart to put it in her cinemas. By the time I got up to the Edinburgh Film Festival, extra performances were being arranged and the box office agreed to cash a cheque so that I could pay for the taxi that had brought me from the airport. Carole Myer gave a tape to Donna Gigliotti with the words 'You won't want this.' Donna bought the film for what seemed like a prince's ransom. In fact her partners had seen the film play to a cheering audience in Toronto. I discovered the film had opened in England because in Calcutta I bought a copy of the *New Statesman* and read a review ('Hanif Kureishi may not be able to spell but he can certainly write'). It went on to play successfully around the world, in Paris, in Spain, in New York. Someone told me Paul Newman queued to see the film.

I feel like a taxi driver who's had a baby born in the back of his cab and had to work as a midwife. Making *My Beautiful Laundrette* was joyful, messy, alive; there was no epidural, no blood-letting, no episiotomy. I had no idea the baby would grow up to be the most successful company in the history of British cinema. What larks!

I remember being invited to an early screening of *My Beautiful Laundrette* at BAFTA when the film was still a TV film and, on Stephen's insistence, was scheduled to go out on Channel 4 without a theatrical release. Carole Myer, who was then working for Channel 4 Sales, was trying to persuade Stephen to let the film have a theatrical release. Carole hoped, and she was right, that many of us in that audience would support her case. The film played to great acclaim at both the Edinburgh and Toronto festivals and became Channel 4's first big theatrical success.
**– Simon Relph, Producer**

## GORDON WARNECKE
Actor, *My Beautiful Laundrette*

*Laundrette* was the first film I had worked on and I am very proud that it still seems to hold its own in British film history. At the time none of us knew that it would have a cinematic release and go on to make such an impact with the public and critics. The actual filming was quite fast but great to do, the crew and cast all pulling together. Stephen Frears was the ideal actor's director as he allowed us to shape the scenes ourselves. We were not dictated to by the camera. For me, watching the likes of Daniel, Rita Woolf and Roshan Seth was an eye-opener into film acting as they are all great actors and know how to deliver. Hanif stayed in the backround during the filming but was always on hand to answer any questions. I don't think he's ever bought me a drink but he's very forthcoming when it comes to his text.

One of my first meetings with Dan was in a Soho coffee shop, we both caught each other out eyeing up a woman in tight leather trousers – without saying anything we just laughed and forgot about the inevitable love scenes. Come the day of the scene when we had to strip down to our waists and make whoopee we just took a mouthful of Listerine each, shut our eyes and thought of England.

The scene that will always stay with me is where I defended my (screen) father, pronouncing him a socialist, not a communist. My own father (who was German) was a socialist for thirty years and was heavily involved within the west London branch of the Socialist Party. Over the years I understood the difference between the two and understood his beliefs so when it came to that scene I knew exactly where Omar was coming from. This is also a mark of how good a writer Hanif is.

Once it came out on video my mum (South American – by now you've probably sussed I'm not exactly the full ticket when it comes to playing a Pakistani) stopped having coffee mornings and, much to my embarrassment, was having *Laundrette* video mornings with her friends. My son, Daniel, who is ten, recently saw a clip of me snogging Daniel Day-Lewis on television. Having never seen the film before he covered his eyes and said he liked me much more in *Brookside*. You can't win them all.

## HANS ZIMMER
Composer, *My Beautiful Laundrette*

Before I sold out to Hollywood, I was Stanley Myers' assistant/alibi when *My Beautiful Laundrette* somehow landed on his doorstep as a project in need of a composer. Even though he was probably the most radically thinking older person I knew at the time and probably the best film composer I've ever known, I don't think he really had a handle on what to do with this tale of immigrants and punks in a Thatcher-infected England. Oh, and there was the gay thing, wasn't there? But whatever the politics of the film, he was also double-booked and we couldn't let on to anyone. To admit the situation would have put him in breach of contract with whatever Hollywood studio he'd made his Faustian pact with this time.

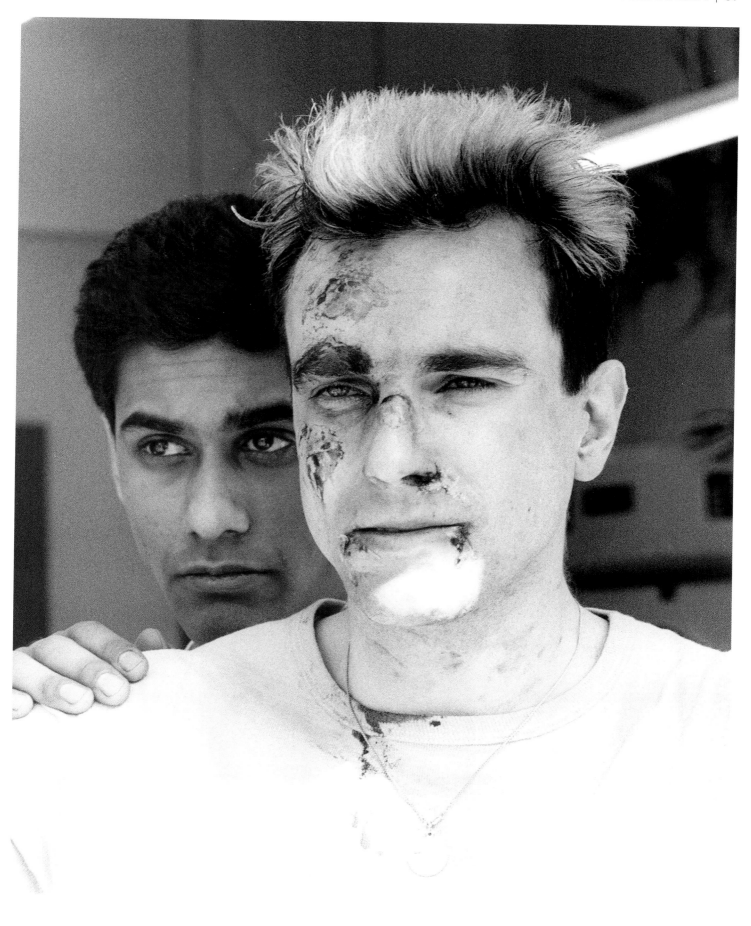

For years, I was convinced by Stanley's rhetoric that you truly sold your soul to Hollywood; that dark and fearsome Mephistopheles-like forces were at work there, and, like Big Brother, they would take account for every second of your life while you were on their payroll for the so-called 'exclusive period' of your contract. Anyway, all of these mysterious goings on in Stanley's life opened up a perfect window of opportunity for his assistant to be given a chance to score *My Beautiful Laundrette* for Working Title – and what better company to be working for on my first outing? The rumours led me to believe they had even less of an idea of how to make a movie than I did, *Laundrette* being their first movie as well as mine. So our plan, since we suspected Working Title wouldn't know the difference between a football score and a film score anyway, was for Stanley to 'supervise' me while finishing his artistically corrupt yet bank account-enlarging endeavour, and for me to not ruin the project, saving him from having to write anything.

Now, this was all happening backstage, so to speak, and I hadn't seen a frame of the movie or met any of the people at Working Title. Stanley came along with me to the first screening, which was in some tiny, dingy room over a porn shop or strip club somewhere in Soho. All the Working Title films I was ever involved with were edited above some sort of seedy sex establishment, yet it was somehow comforting for me to know that, even though our movie-making had risen a few steps above, we were still clearly connected to a simpler bit of showbiz that was going on downstairs. It's always important to have your eye on another market should the director reject your score.

I seem to remember that Stanley was really taken by what we saw in that screening – this wasn't the sort of movie we were used to. This wasn't a BBC period drama or some Hollywood piece of fluff; this felt like it was about real people and real life. *My Beautiful Laundrette* actually had something to say about the England of 1985, and it was delivered in a sort of gritty passion more akin to The Clash than Merchant Ivory. The people involved in the film definitely matched the style of the piece itself: Stephen Frears, the director; Hanif Kureishi, the writer; Mick Audsley, our great editor, who could speak eloquently about music; and, of course, Sarah Radclyffe and Tim Bevan, the producers. There seemed to be no real rank or one-upmanship; everyone was trying to do what was best for the movie. And there was chaos – something I always embrace wholeheartedly.

Stanley pretty much decided there and then that maybe this film was a little bit too good to completely hand over to the assistant after all, and instead it truly became a writing partnership between the two of us. Looking back, I think *Laundrette* was probably the best collaboration we had together, and I think a large reason for this was linked to the spirit Working Title brings to all of their projects. To this day, I feel there's a tone in a Working Title film that comes from the personalities and presence of those involved in the company, although their sense of aesthetics is never forced upon the project: it's more like a group of like-minded explorers finding their way through the uncharted territory of a film together. And there's a sense of friendship; you work openly and daringly with the license to make courageous choices in an environment where nobody makes you feel foolish if some of your more wacky ideas went a bit pear-shaped. So it was perhaps no accident that *My Beautiful Laundrette* turned into a strange cultural phenomenon, capturing the zeitgeist of an England that the established filmmakers ignored.

*Laundrette* was one of those miraculous productions where one knew that everything – the writing, the acting and the direction – magically hung together in the balance.
**– Saeed Jaffrey, Actor**

Working with Shirley Anne Field was great. Especially as my dad admitted he used to drool over her in the 60s and 70s. When I introduced her to him at the premiere, it was the first time I ever saw him lost for words! I have to admit she is a classy bird!
**– Gordon Warnecke, Actor**

*Opposite:* **Nasser (Saeed Jaffrey) and Rachel (Shirley Anne Field) dance in the Laundrette**

**Linda (Emily Lloyd) cycles along the promenade at Worthing in *Wish You Were Here***

# DAVID LELAND
## Writer and Director, *Wish You Were Here*

My first recollections of Working Title were of Sarah Radclyffe and her team sitting in one room in an office just off Coptic Street near the British Museum. It was next to a Pizza Express and the smell of pizzas baking permeated into the office. Everyone worked round a large table, so everything was open. There was no need for staff meetings because the working day was one large staff meeting, everyone was party to every call and conversation and knew what was going on. It generated a high energy and sometimes a frantic atmosphere that was exciting to be around.

I wrote *Wish You Were Here* more or less by accident. At the time I was attempting to write *Personal Services*, a film about Cynthia Payne, who had been prosecuted for running a brothel from her home in Streatham in south London. *Wish You Were Here* began as a story about Cynthia's early years but became equally if not more about my own memories of growing up in a village near Cambridge which had its own bowling club, British Legion culture and a beautiful young girl who rode round the village green on her bike with the wind in her skirt.

Having written *Personal Services* I then put myself up as director for *Wish You Were Here*. David Rose, the Head of Drama at Channel 4, knew both my writing and my work as a director at the Crucible Theatre in Sheffield and instantly backed my bid to direct on film. We started with a budget of £750,000 to shoot on 16mm for TV, but Sarah was ambitious to make and release it as a cinematic feature and managed to double the budget to £1.5 million so that we got a longer shooting schedule (six weeks) and shot it on 35mm.

The general opinion was that we would have to cast somewhat older than fifteen years for the character of Linda. I didn't agree with this, but was uncertain we would find someone the right age who could play the part. We screen tested five young women, all between seventeen and nineteen, except for Emily who was only fifteen. Emily had a somewhat gauche style of moving and acting which looked uncoordinated to the eye but was somehow transfomed by the camera. In the middle of viewing her screen test, the editor, George Akers, leaned over and whispered in my ear, 'The camera likes her'. And it did. But her performance was not as easily or naturally achieved as it appears on screen. We rehearsed hard and with each take I threw in added elements with which Emily always coped, even when things went disastrously wrong. Our only rule was, 'DON'T STOP'. And she never did. She had great determination and spirit, as well as talent.

Sarah and the Working Title team were very aware of the need to put a support structure around such a young performer. In each department Sarah employed people she thought Emily would like and feel at home with. It worked. Although it was not until later, when Emily went to work on other films, that I suspect she discovered this doesn't usually happen.

# EMILY LLOYD
## Actress, *Wish You Were Here*

I was having lunch with David Leland, when he asked me if I would like to play the character of Linda in the film. I remember replying yes and laughing nervously, not realizing the implication of his question. Then he said, 'You've got the part' and the spoonful of soup I had just put into my mouth splattered on to the table and I felt a huge surge of happiness. My fifteen-year-old expectations of life had just been given wings.

While working on the film, I experienced many magical moments and images that will always stay with me: cycling along the grey seafront in Worthing, the steel railings which gave me strength as I leant on them, learning the art of flirting with Brian (played by Lee Whitlock). The feelings of serenity, strolling past the still lake pushing a pram in my yellow dress, in harmony with David's gentle direction, bonding with the rest of the cast and crew. So many good memories. Most of the scenes were shot in chronological order, apart from the last day of filming. David had decided to keep the seduction scene with Tom Bell until the end of filming as he and Tom were both sensitive about the content and my reaction to it. I remember calling my mother and telling her not to be concerned about me shooting the delicate scene as I was at ease living in Linda's world and knowing her character. David gave me the stability, which at sixteen years old I needed. He harnessed my talent, understood me and gave me the inspiration to bring Linda to life and know her spirit. He is a brilliant director and I feel the success of the film was primarily due to him.

*Wish You Were* Here was selected for the Cannes Film Festival and I was invited to attend. I felt as if I had been transported into an exhilarating, stimulating but unreal world. My days consisted of a whirl of photocalls and interviews. I was also chosen to present flowers to Princess Diana. She was very beautiful and had the warmest of smiles. I had wanted to wear a black mini-skirt for the presentation but was firmly told that this would not be appropriate for the occasion. I was rather peeved about this at the time as I thought a teenager should be able to wear what she liked! Another day, during my stay there, I was slightly taken aback when an aeroplane circling the blue skies of Cannes came into my view. A banner was attached to the plane displaying the words in large letters 'We Love Emily'. I really wanted to be sitting next to the pilot!

**Keeping your lead actress quiet!**

My first day on set happened to be my sixteenth birthday and there was a wonderful sense of excitement in the air. The cameraman, Ian Wilson, who unbeknownst to me was the jester on the set, asked me if I liked chocolate cake. His facial expression amused me as he realized he had inadvertently let it slip that there was a chocolate cake and a birthday party arranged for me later that day. It was an unforgettable birthday.
**– Emily Lloyd, Actress**

**David on Emily**
**'How to pose like Betty Grable'**
We shot this scene on the seafront at
Worthing, it was one of the first
scenes to be shot. Emily had never
heard of Betty Grable. Linda, Emily's
character, strikes the Betty Grable
pose to show off her goods and to
attract the attention of boys on the
promenade. We put a giant Betty
Grable cut-out outside the Dome
cinema in Worthing, which features as
a location in the film. This beautiful old
cinema was under threat of
demolition to become a car park and
filming there helped to preserve it.
**– David Leland, Director**

**Brian (Lee Whitlock, left) and
Cinematographer Ian Wilson
(far right) look on as David
Leland puts Linda (Emily Lloyd)
through her paces**

**Emily on David**

The photograph was taken on my first day of filming *Wish You Were Here*, aged just sixteen. My very first experience of becoming a professional actress. Due to my naivety, I was unaware that a photographer was clicking away on his camera while I had been thinking it was a private moment between director and actress, or teacher and pupil! The photograph illustrates David showing me the art of female seduction, how a simple contrived move can attract the opposite sex. My introduction to the mating ritual has served me well! Riding the bicycle along the Worthing seafront gave me the feeling of liberation and fun that was part of Linda's personality. I have no recollection of feeling nervous during the first day on the set, just pure excitement at entering into the world of creativity.
– Emily Lloyd, Actress

**Terry Jones and Tim Bevan get into character on the set of *Personal Services***

Throughout the filming, I remember Tim permanently wearing a sublime schoolboy grin, just as he appears in the photograph with director Terry Jones. In the photo, it's immediately noticeable that Terry is chained to the wall by his neck; but what is less obvious is that Tim is holding a 'spanking paddle', an instrument used by the dominatrix to keep errant clients in place. Every producer should have one.
— **David Leland, Writer**

# DAVID LELAND
## Writer, *Personal Services*

*Personal Services* was inspired by the charitable works of Cynthia Payne, she of the luncheon voucher brothel scandal, a life turned to legend in the courtrooms of England, and later a parliamentary candidate for the Pleasure and Payne Party. *Personal Services* is everything I experienced in the good company of Cynthia Payne and her friends. It is a portrait of her world.

Making *Personal Services* was more an event than a shoot. The sexual incongruities of Cynthia's life transferred exquisitely to the set; actors, particularly the men, took great delight in dressing up in bikinis, baby-doll nighties and gym slips; or being clad in rubber and trapped into a DIY punishment chair. Mysteriously, the number of soft-porn magazines dressed on the set by the art department increased as people brought in samples from their own collections to add to what became an increasingly hard-core pile.

From the time Tim Bevan began producing the film, he made the point of calling me two or three times a week, sometimes more, to strategize on putting the film together. We discussed actors, directors, designers, everything. He showed great sensitivity, knowing that if he got it right at the beginning then it would work through to the end.

As the writer, trying to keep a low profile on the set, I appeared in drag in the big sex party scene looking rather spookily like Myra Hindley. I tried to persuade Bevan to do the same but, as much as he delighted in what was going on around him, he refused to don a frock. A natural born voyeur, I suspect. On the last day of filming the plan was to finish early and decamp as quickly as possible to Streatham where Cynthia was throwing a party for the crew, together with a gathering of her most trusted and devoted clients, ladies and friends. As it happened, the shoot went on past eleven at night which meant that we unfortunately missed the police raid on the party that led to nine charges against Cynthia under Section 31 of the 1956 Sexual Offences Act. The crew had missed both party and police but, by some fluke of timing, numerous members of the press had somehow managed to arrive on Cynthia's doorstep fifteen minutes before the raid began. It made headline news.

Had the nine charges stuck, Cynthia could have been given seven years; as it was, she was acquitted and the trial which kept the nation amused for the duration, became the most glorious piece of free publicity for our film. We later learnt that the tip-off for the raid had come from two undercover policemen who had beavered away at Cynthia's parties for over fifteen months disguised in women's clothes, in the hope of putting an incriminating finger on Madame Cyn. As it happened, I was at some of the same parties as these two undercover 'trannie' cops. This leaves me rather perplexed as I failed to spot either of them. Although, when I come to think of it, I do remember a man with a striking resemblance to Doberman from *Sergeant Bilko* wearing a full-length black velvet skirt with a frilly white cotton Laura Ashley blouse. (It's heartening to know they can be found in such large sizes.) But I still cannot recall either of them for certain — unless, of course, one of them happened to look like the glorious Doberman. Had I known that, I might have been tempted. I wonder if they took their disguises home with them at night?

# HUGO LUCZYC-WYHOWSKI
## Production Designer, *Personal Services*

I had a strange but unique perspective sat on the flowery chenille sofa at number 32, Ambleside Avenue. Surely this wasn't real research for the set? Was I day dreaming? After half an hour of questions, Cynthia [Payne] was rambling on about Slave Peter's gardening abilities. The plaster cherubs grinned cheekily from their bed on the beige woodchip wallpaper. The carpet swirled slowly around the coffee table legs. Two scrambled egg and salad cream finger rolls were left on the pearl-effect plate.

'So what exactly is that six-foot length of timber with loops at either end doing suspended from a pulley in your conservatory?' I asked politely.

'That's where we do the bank manager,' said Cynthia enthusiastically.

'Do the bank manager?'

'Yes, we do him in the conservatory 'cos there's tiles on the floor and it's easy to clean up the mess.' She smiled.

Cynthia had toured me all around her house. The closet containing the 500 pairs of high heels, the beds all neatly made with their candlewick spreads. The kitchen where the famous tea and poachies were administered après ski. The special door bell entry sequence of three rings had been explained, as well as the accounting system for luncheon vouchers and extra credits. I had been shown all the photo albums as well as the postcards. I had even carefully noted the little handwritten sign sellotaped over the wash basin in the bathroom: 'No fucking on the basin, someone pulled it off the wall last Thursday'.

And now did I really want to find out about the mess? It seems there was no choice.

'Yes he's a funny fellow that manager.'

'What exactly do you mean Cyn?' I offered.

'He likes to be degraded and it makes a bit of a mess. We string him up by the hands and then he likes to be covered with raspberry jam and hoover fluff!'

On *Personal Services* we greatly enjoyed exploring the solid British character actor fraternity in order to cast a variety of sex slaves and fetishists.
**– Michelle Guish,
Casting Director**

**Christine Painter (Julie Walters) makes her clients tea and poachies après ski, in *Personal Services***
The Wing Commander and Alec McCowen (seated, far right) LOVE Julie Walters. She kept us all happy, all through *Personal Services*.
**– Alec McCowen, Actor**

**Stephen Frears (left) and Tim Bevan on the set of *Sammy and Rosie Get Laid***

After *Laundrette* we also supported *Sammy and Rosie Get Laid*. It's a complicated night shoot, involving a couple of hundred extras and a load of horses – rioters clashing with riot police. Cars explode, one after the other, and a sheet of flame tears across a row of shops. Tim is pacing up and down, looking rather less urbane than usual and muttering something about insurance which I think I probably don't want to hear. Hanif is standing by a smouldering car, and as I come up to him he turns with a look of wonder on his face and says – 'All I wrote was one little line – "there is rioting in the street"'.

**– Karin Bamborough, Channel 4 1981–90**

**Rosie (Frances Barber) stands outside Danny's caravan in** *Sammy and Rosie Get Laid*
We filmed this scene in February in the bitter cold under the Westway in London. It was supposed to be the morning after a night of bliss with Roland Gift. The photo ended up on the poster for the film all over the Underground. All I remember is being absolutely freezing and wishing I had been wrapped up in a huge coat or Roland's arms.
**– Frances Barber, Actress**

# GRAHAM BRADSTREET
Finance Director, Working Title Films 1986-92

**First lengthy telephone call from Tim:**
**TB:** I hear you're an accountant.
**GB:** Yes.
**TB:** We should meet.
**GB:** OK. (Time and place arranged.)
No social niceties. No points of reference. No background.

It later transpired that Nic Roeg (with whom I was attempting to finance *Castaway*) had recommended Tim call me as it was obvious he needed an accountant. After several meetings with Tim, we agreed that I would assist him in financing Working Title's films.

**TB:** Oh – you should meet Sarah, as she will have to OK you.
**GB:** Who is Sarah?
**TB:** My business partner. (She had not previously been mentioned.)
**GB:** Oh. OK then.

The meeting with Sarah couldn't have been more different. Lots of social niceties. Lots of points of reference. Lots of background.

Together they had just produced *My Beautiful Laundrette*. Sarah had completed *Caravaggio* and was starting *Wish You Were Here*, whilst Tim was trying to close *Personal Services*. I had raised some finance and been production accountant on a couple of films. However, on the back of the above-mentioned works with their artistic and commercial integrity, we raised £250,000 of development money. This did give Working Title control and ownership of its product – despite eventually losing all the development money. No bank was interested nor believed we would produce the proposed slate until we found Alexander Gelderman at what was then Mees Pierson. His commitment to Working Title was beyond the call of duty; we would never have thrived without Alexander's understanding of Working Title and the three of us.

We also got lucky with *Sammy And Rosie Get Laid*. With Hanif and Stephen, Tim and Sarah repeating the *Laundrette* package, the film was fully financed in less than six weeks. As this became the benchmark for getting things done, it was harder work and downhill all the way thereafter. In fact it was always hard work. Hard finding decent product. Hard finding financing. Hard producing. Hard constantly deferring fees. Hard not to lose money.

There was, however, enormous camaraderie with fellow independents, particularly Nik Powell and Steve Woolley, Roger Randall Cutler, Margaret Matheson and Scott Meek. Simon Relph at British Screen and Colin Leventhal at Channel 4 had wide doors and supported us whenever possible.

Hard work and luck kept us going – oh, and personal commitment to each other – no matter how bleak or vibrant the situation. Despite, or even perhaps because of this, PolyGram bought us – but that's for someone else to tell.

*Opposite above:* **Rosie Hobbs (Frances Barber) and Danny (Roland Gift) share an intimate moment on the set of *Sammy and Rosie Get Laid***
Roland and I are actually chatting to each other for real in this shot. It was captured by the stills photographer as we were waiting for the next set-up. I can't remember what he was saying to me, but looking at it now, it looks quite dirty whatever it was. I love the look on the (real) policemen's faces in the background. I think their expressions speak volumes…
**– Frances Barber, Actress**

*Opposite below:* **Danny (Roland Gift) in front of his caravan**

**Diana Roth (Barbara Hershey) and Molly Roth (Jodhi May) at an ANC Rally in *A World Apart*** This is by far, one of my favourite films that I've ever been involved with. I love the intimate questions it raises. Is Diana not there for her children because she uses herself up helping the world? Or is she drawn to that work because she's afraid of intimacy? I also love that in dealing with apartheid, the film was made before Mandela was released.

**– Barbara Hershey, Actress**

# CHRIS MENGES
Director, *A World Apart*

I owe so much to Working Title – they afforded me the best opportunity of my career. If I had to choose only one film to direct or shoot in my lifetime *A World Apart* would be the one.

I had been in South Africa in 1963, working for *World In Action* to report on apartheid, the police state and the ninety-day detention law, So I knew the score – as a naive twenty-two year-old, wielding a Bolex camera! We had travelled north, trying with some success to make contact with ANC units, our journey took us across the border into Matabeleland, Zimbabwe, and the wide streets of the city of Bulawayo.

In 1987 Sarah Radclyffe asked me to direct *A World Apart.* I knew that this was the directing opportunity I had been waiting for, but I also knew that we both wouldn't and couldn't shoot in South Africa and that Bulawayo was the city to stand in for Johannesburg. Not only did it have the right elements of an industrial city but the people of Matabeleland had been fierce supporters of the ANC during its bitter fight for freedom and, as a result, we were able to cast the film and be inspired and advised by people who had actually lived the reality. The dream of every filmmaker is to work in collaboration with people who know the truth and to create an engine to fire the shoot. Thanks to Shawn Slovo's moving story and tremendous script, and the fine work of crew and cast, we all made a film to be proud of.

The film critic Pauline Kael liked the film a great deal but admonished me for 'not trusting the audience' by ending on a clenched fist. She said the film had already shown apartheid as evil.

That much-maligned clenched fist! It says united together we will win, but we are not winning. Right now millions of Ndebile-speaking people are being terrorised and starved in Matabeleland. Why is its democratic big brother, across the border, ignoring this nightmare?

**Jodhi May with Chris Menges on the set of *A World Apart***
I remember the day this picture was taken, Chris had asked me to find a spot where I could have a quiet moment alone and then he vanished. Then suddenly he appeared whispering in my ear before the take, and vanished again. That was the scene. I had no idea where the camera was, it was an intimate moment and Chris instinctively caught the reality of the moment as it unfolded.
**– Jodhi May, Actress**

## SHAWN SLOVO
*Writer, A World Apart*

In 1986, I wrote *A World Apart*, my first script, as a screenwriting student at the National Film and Television School. There was a certain amount of interest from the film industry in Britain, but when Sarah Radclyffe and Tim Bevan expressed an interest, there was no hesitation on my part in giving them the option. They were young, hip and good-looking, fresh off the successes of *My Beautiful Laundrette* and *Wish You Were Here*, and their enthusiasm for the script was exhilarating. In those days, they worked out of a one-room office in Livonia Street, with an assistant between them and maybe a runner, and the atmosphere was relaxed and informal.

Above all, they were respectful of the script, and inclusive. I was made to feel part of the team, consulted at every stage of pre- and post-production, on location with the cast and crew for the whole period of shooting in Zimbabwe.

We celebrated in style when the film was selected as an official entry to the 1987 Cannes Film Festival. We doubled up in bedrooms and queued for the bathroom in the flat we stayed in, partied hard and loose, linked arms as we made our way up the red carpet, and left Cannes in triumph a collective wreck.

*A World Apart* established me as a screenwriter, and for a few years in the 1990s I started working for the American majors, getting caught up in the development hell which is the fate for many screenwriters at one time or another in their careers. When I hooked up again with Working Title after that baptism of fire, it felt like coming home. Although Sarah was no longer part of the company, this relationship forged in the 1980s has persevered with Tim, and developed with Eric, to the present.

**Chris Menges with writer Shawn Slovo on the set of *A World Apart***
I remember the brilliant long shadows of a day at work; the special fragrance of Africa, and the joy of collaboration. I miss the company of Joe Slovo, and Ruth, who I did not know, but often thought about.
**– Chris Menges, Director**

# HANS ZIMMER
## Composer, *A World Apart*

*A World Apart* was my first truly solo outing as a film composer, and I remember the great trouble Sarah Radclyffe went to, to persuade Chris Menges to give me the job. I finally had a meeting with him at a lunch Sarah had engineered. It wasn't until the end of lunch I summoned enough courage to ask him if I shouldn't just write a piece of music as a demo track for one of the scenes. He eagerly agreed. I labored for days on this piece, and it became the most subtle, quiet and fragile little jewel, which I nervously brought over to the cutting rooms.

Chris said 'Well, let's give it a listen', and the editor threaded the mag-machine up to the scene. I knew I was doomed as soon as he hit play. His machine had the most god-awful howl that overpowered the music I'd written – you couldn't hear a note through the whine and scrape of the motors. It was the closest I ever came to hearing the sound of a mechanical donkey baying. Chris never got to hear the piece I'd written for him, but he gave me the film anyway, I suspect, because he felt so sorry for me. Some weeks later, he cut the whole scene.

Like all Working Title films of that time, the music budget on *A World Apart* was miniscule. This had the positive side effect that you were forced into being inventive. This can be very exciting, because you have to write something that's inspired, appropriate to the film itself, deeply honest and emotional, but can translate well to being performed on a rubber band stretched over an old cardboard box. The downside to this situation is that in addition to the normal creative pressures, I had no idea how to make the project work financially, and there wasn't any room for error.

*Back row left to right:* **The Roth family: Gus Roth (Jeroen Krabbé), Molly Roth (Jodhi May), Diana Roth (Barbara Hershey),** *Front row:* **Miriam Roth (Carolyn Clayton-Cragg) and Jude Roth (Merav Grauer)**

I remember that towards the end of *A World Apart*, after all the money had been spent and all the musicians had gone home, Chris brought over a small reel of tape that his wife Judy had recorded in Africa under very difficult circumstances – and naturally this was the only copy and really quite irreplaceable. We took one listen to it and instantly knew this had to become the inspiration for our end-title music, so I asked my sound engineer, Al Clay, to erase the music we had recorded with the orchestra to force me into really committing to the African piece. The orchestra piece was good, but this new African idea could be great!

Sure enough, Al put all the tracks into record and basically erased my – or rather, our – safety net. There was no going back, but I felt this was a decision very much in the spirit of the Working Title 'reckless yet committed' approach I'd seen all around me. As soon as the old track was wiped, Chris asked to hear the African piece just one more time. I put the tape machine into rewind, and it promptly mangled the tape – the one and only tape, remember – into the motors with the same ease and menacing nature of a waste disposal machine. No one other than Al and I knew what had happened, and Chris was left wondering why we weren't playing the music back. I can't remember what we told him, but after he left, we sat on the floor of the studio all night splicing literally thousands of tape fragments back together again. Somehow we got it done, and it really became a wonderful piece of music.

After we finished the movie, it was selected as an official entry into the Cannes film festival, so Cannes was going to be our premiere. Cannes is important. It's about great filmmaking and art, but Cannes is also very much about selling and power too. The really filthy rich stay there on yachts moored in the harbour; those who are just very rich, but still really big and powerful, stay at the Hotel du Cap; and the next echelon down enjoy the hospitality of the Carlton, where all the major studios have their offices. However, attending the Cannes Film Festival in Working Title style that year meant seven of us staying in a two-bedroom apartment in the industrial outskirts of Cannes.

While the festival doesn't specify the level of glamour for the accommodation of its attendees, there's a requirement that filmmakers must be chauffeured in big black stretch limos to the red carpet for the premiere of their film, which wasn't exactly Working Title style that year. So to attend our premiere, we all got dressed up, hiked across town for a good half-hour to the hotel Martinez, which is situated right on the opposite side of the street from the red carpet, piled into the limos, did a swift U-turn and got out.

There was a photo of us all marching up the red carpet in one of the English papers. I love that photo, because it captures the moment where we still didn't know if the movie was going to play to an audience, and the anxiety of this is right there in the crooked smiles of that shot. Just because we loved the film didn't necessarily mean it would touch the audience – it's like putting your defenceless child on a stage and hoping the crowd will be kind, rather than cruel and hurtful. And all the people who were there with you, who'd been involved in making the movie, were, at that moment, closer to you than your real family; they were your brothers in arms. It was no longer about whether my music would shine, but that we had all stayed up for many nights working and worrying alone or together. We were at Cannes together in that moment because of each other, this small band camping in some dive, who weren't really part of the glitzy movie crowd or the beautiful people of Hollywood. We were intruders, and in a few minutes we'd find out if maybe we were imposters as well, that we didn't have what it takes to make a movie soar. As the film got underway, however, I started to feel the excitement you only get from a great film connecting with an audience – that great and wonderful shared experience when you know the audience is not just with the movie, but part of it. To this day, I've never had a better experience at a premiere. It was as if I could feel each individual member of the audience, as if the movie was told back to me by all the people around me, and I saw stories and emotions buried in the film that I could never have seen by myself until I'd seen them through their eyes. I've been back to Cannes many times, I've stayed at the Hotel du Cap, and I've partied on the yachts; but the experience has never been as good as the time when I was there with a Working Title film.

**The moving funeral procession in *A World Apart***

**The Tall Guy: An elongated Jeff Goldblum as Dexter King**

**Richard Curtis outside the 'Elephant!' theatre**
O God. I used to wonder why I entered the apparently glamorous world of movies and it made absolutely no difference to my non-existent love-life. Here at last is the answer – the diamond pattern jumper, too hideous for even Frank Bough, even Alan Partridge – the big glasses – the bigger hair. Please don't include this in the book.
**– Richard Curtis, Writer**

# RICHARD CURTIS
Writer, *The Tall Guy*

**The Tall Guy was your first film. How did the script happen?**
By 1987, I had already had the benign, but traumatizing experience of writing a film for an American film producer in the US. After months of work, I was staying in the producer's house and had a big meeting with a charming executive from MGM, who said, 'We absolutely love your script – the only things we don't like are the two main characters, the dialogue, the jokes and the cameos'. I said, 'That only leaves the title'. She added, 'And we wanted to talk to you about the title…'. I knew I'd never get the film finished, let alone made.

And quite right too – the movie was set in Boston and I was on incredibly shaky ground. So when I returned from America, I vowed only to write films that were set somewhere where I knew every single geographical and actual detail. So I wrote *Camden Town Boy* (as it was then called) which was, with huge exaggeration, about my experiences as Rowan's [Atkinson] straight man in the West End. It was also about a man with hay fever and a nurse – and I also had hayfever in those days and went for regular injections to a hospital on Hampstead Road, where I had a crush on a nurse who I only ever saw when she was injecting me.

**How did you end up at Working Title?**
I finished the script and my agent Anthony Jones told me to go to Working Title and see Tim Bevan. Crucial good piece of advice. Tim read the script, liked it, and worked out a way to finance the film pretty well exclusively from the sale of the TV rights. When I asked him how he sold the script to people (looking for a compliment I expect), he said, 'I never mentioned the script, I just showed them it couldn't make a loss'. Then, extraordinarily, because I think he trusted the script and trusted me, he said 'Who would you like to direct it?'. I had no idea at all – but I did remember that when we finished *Not the Nine O'Clock News*, Mel Smith had told me, 'If ever you write a film and I don't direct it, I'll kill you'. So I thought, 'Why risk my life?'. So we asked Mel to direct it, with Paul Webster as producer. There wasn't much at stake financially, and I think Tim was already in the frame of mind that has often served Working Title so well, which is to trust the people they're working with to know what's right for them.

**How did you end up with Jeff Goldblum as the leading man?**
We had fun casting the smaller parts, but just couldn't find our leading man. If Hugh had been on the scene, I would probably have rejected him on the same grounds that I wanted to reject him on *Four Weddings* – too posh and too good looking. There were a couple of British actors I wanted that Mel and I couldn't agree on, so as a joke I said if I couldn't have those two, I wanted either Jeff Goldblum or Judge Reinhold. Mel took me up on it, and sent the script to Jeff – who claims he read it aloud in bed to his then wife Geena, who laughed a lot – so he said 'yes'.

**And Emma Thompson – it was her first film, wasn't it?**
It was obvious from the first second of Emma Thompson's screen test, that she should play the part. At that time, I only knew her as a sketch performer, but when we screen-tested her with three other girls, there was this blinding moment when she first came on screen. I'd never seen her even trying to do proper acting and then suddenly there she was, being a completely extraordinary screen actress – which she has remained until this day.

### Was making it a happy experience?

Yes – very – I think because of the modesty of our set-up and ambitions. Mel and I knew each other well, a lot of the cast were friends, and we didn't have much money – most of the music is sound-alikes – my friends Philip Pope is both the Everly Brothers and Long John Baldry. Also I was given enormous leeway by Tim from the very beginning and Mel was completely happy that I should be on set all the time. If he saw me frantic at the end of a take, he would say to me, 'Okay – let's just do a take of what you want and we'll see.' The terrible thing, of course, is that, after feeling insanely passionately about how right I was, often when we watched the rushes back, I couldn't even see which were my takes.

### When it was finished – did you test it a lot?

Quite a lot. Even in those early days, I was very open to testing a film with an audience. Our stage shows had in effect been 'screen tested': you did them on day one, then cut the bits that didn't work and added bits where it was working well. And sitcoms are almost a live performance – where once again you cut the bits that the studio audience don't laugh at.

### How did the tests go?

The film tested pretty well in the UK. But when we took it to the US to test, it was like watching it underwater – total silence – Jacques Cousteau presents *The Tall Guy*. I remember the two car journeys with the Weinstein Brothers (Harvey and Bob), our North American distributors. On the way to the screening, they were planning to release the film in 300 cinemas moving up to 1,000. On the way back, after zero laughs, they somewhat revised their figures. 'Well, let's start at two – just one per coast – and see if it goes up from there.' It didn't.

### So generally a good experience?

Very good. It was a naive part of our lives, when we thought we could just make a film, and hope for the best. And didn't really care too much.

Producing *The Tall Guy*. For Richard Curtis, Emma Thompson, Rowan Atkinson and Mel Smith it is their introduction to the film business. Watching Mel, generously allowing Richard to have 'his take' after he is comfortable that he has what he needs in the can. Watching Richard fuss over the exact patterns of the ties that Jeff Goldblum would use to tie Rowan to a chair and wondering if this is what attention to detail means or am I watching some compulsive obsessive at work?
**– Paul Webster, Producer**

**Elephant! The Musical: The Elephant Dance from *The Tall Guy***

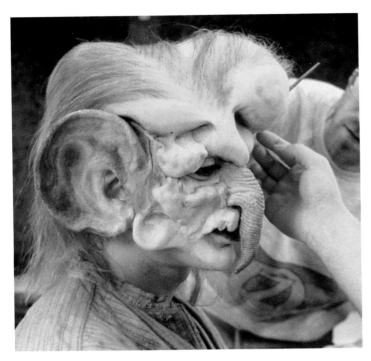

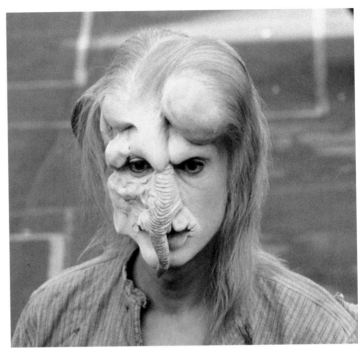

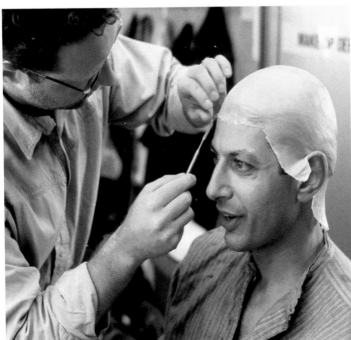

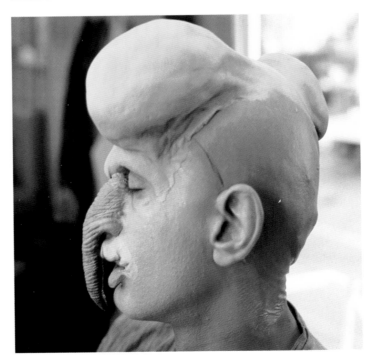

**Jeff Goldblum has his prosthetic
Elephant Man make-up applied
in *The Tall Guy***

**Kate Lemmon (Emma Thompson) and Dexter King (Jeff Goldblum) deface the poster of Ron Anderson (Rowan Atkinson) outside his West End theatre in *The Tall Guy***

Jeff was fantastic and bonkers. He used to read P. G. Wodehouse to me in a very bad English accent before every take until I took away the book and threw it at him.
**– Emma Thompson, Actress**

# INITIAL FILMS

SID AND NANCY
PASCALI'S ISLAND
HIDDEN AGENDA
A KISS BEFORE DYING

# ROGER DEAKINS
Cinematographer, *Sid and Nancy*

My relationship with Eric Fellner, Tim Bevan and Working Title started in the early 1980s with *Sid and Nancy* and continues to this day. The making of the movie, about the punk band The Sex Pistols, at times seemed a recreation of the gritty reality we were attempting to put on the screen. Eric produced the film and it was an example of guerilla filmmaking at its best. We didn't have much money (and that is an understatement!) but Eric ensured that every penny of our scant budget showed up on the screen.

This was not a film with star trailers and executive privileges. We were a very small crew and Eric was an integral part. When eight of us flew to Paris to grab shots, Eric was one of that number. He carried his share of the equipment as we ran from one recognizable location to another to steal shots. We were back in London after a night shoot at the Moulin Rouge.

We travelled to America for a portion of *Sid and Nancy*, bringing part of our English crew. At that point, most of us were not the seasoned travellers that we are now. We arrived in New York after a very long flight in the late afternoon and immediately launched into a scout that lasted until 9p.m. Although we could barely function at that point, we then sat down for a production meeting. The New York crew had expected a group of inexperienced Brits making a small film that might never see the light of day. They had never heard of Gary Oldman and didn't take us very seriously. I suspect that none of us were making much sense in that meeting. Midway, my exhausted assistant cameraman came into the room and announced that as he was checking out the camera gear, the camera vehicle started leaking diesel fuel. The camera boxes were spread out on the sidewalk and it had just started to snow. And, by the way, he was now going to the hotel. I will never forget leaving that meeting about midnight, walking onto the snowy streets of New York City and seeing our camera gear strewn on the sidewalk as well as about twenty-eight gallons of diesel fuel coming out of the camera truck. Eric and I just looked at each and said, 'Welcome to America!'.

Things continued in this vein. On our first day of production in New York, we were in an industrial area, shooting across at the twin towers. Much to our dismay, we learned that the production manager had not supplied lunch, which was a problem since this was not a neighborhood with restaurants. On top of this, our genny operator threatened to walk if he were not paid up front immediately. Without the power, we would have to shut down before we started! Eric thought quickly and had a 'whip round' the crew, and collected enough money to pay the genny operator and allow us to complete our first day of shooting.

Eric was 'Mr Fix It' on the shoot. We were shooting in the Chelsea Hotel and ran into the age-old problem that often occurs on shoots. The idea of having his hotel in a movie seemed like a good idea to the manager until he encountered the cables and chaos that comprise the reality of a shoot. At that point, he wanted to shut us down and Eric worked wonders every day to keep us shooting. As he would speak soothingly to the manager at one end of the hotel, we would scramble up the back stairs and grab a scene. The tiny size of our crew certainly worked in our favour, making it far easier to sneak around!

There were delays shooting outside of the old CBGB's in NYC. It was past midnight and the holding area for the punk extras was the library of the local school. Eric asked me and Dee Dee Ramone, who was playing the bouncer, to go over there and 'talk to them because they're ripping the books off the shelves and starting fires'. We walked into total chaos. Dee Dee stood on a desk and I introduced him. He waited until it was completely silent, and then he said, 'What are you lookin' for?…LOVE?'. They stared at him for about twenty seconds and then went back to wreaking havoc. Eric laughed and said 'Fuck it, so I'm paying library fines…again'.
— **Chloe Webb, Actress**

**Paris is for lovers: Nancy Spungen (Chloe Webb) and Sid Vicious (Gary Oldman) visit the Eiffel Tower in *Sid and Nancy***

One morning we came up with the idea of the falling garbage cans shot, which is one of the most famous shots in the movie. As we drove to work, the writer, Abbe Wool, suggested that, during the shot when Sid and Nancy kiss, garbage could be falling around them. This evolved into garbage cans. I then said it would have to be shot in slow motion. This meant we had to find a slow-motion camera right away as well as the garbage cans. The only slow-motion camera to be had was one that had definitely seen better days. The magazine frequently jammed and we were constantly reloading the film. We weren't sure we would get enough frames to make the shot, but happily we had one interval between jams that allowed us to get a shot that really worked.

*Sid and Nancy* was an adventure from start to finish. It was an exciting way to make a film and it worked. I often look around today's heavily populated sets and miss those days of shooting from the hip.

*Overleaf:*
**Alex Cox (left) directs Chloe Webb and Gary Oldman**

**Anthony Bowles (Charles Dance) and Lydia Neuman (Helen Mirren) share an intimate moment in** *Pascali's Island*

## JAMES DEARDEN
Director, *Pascali's Island*

I first met Eric some time early in 1987. I had sent my screenplay of *Pascali's Island* to Jeremy Thomas, who had other commitments at the time, but recommended me to this 'very bright, hip young guy called Eric Fellner', whom he predicted (presciently) would one day be a force in the land. I met Eric and liked him immediately, the more so as he was very enthusiastic about the project. I was therefore chagrined when a few weeks later he telephoned to say that regrettably he had too much on his plate and couldn't commit to doing the film that year. I called Jeremy again to ask his advice. 'Why don't you try this other guy, Tim Bevan?' he recommended. I duly had lunch with Tim, who also liked the project and said he'd do it. Then I didn't hear from Tim for a while, and I can't really remember what happened next exactly, except that Eric came back on the scene a few months later and I ended up doing the film with him after all.

*Pascali* proved to be the happiest of experiences in terms of cast, crew, location (Greek island), weather – for once everything that could go right went right. I can still remember the incredible energy and enthusiasm that Eric brought to the enterprise, which filtered through to everyone in the crew, from Roger Deakins and Paul Raphael down, most of whom had worked with him before. No one complained, they worked criminally long hours, and for some – like the 'Crew Sluts', our transportation team – accommodation meant a sleeping bag in a half-completed building. (Unfortunately, after a night of carousing, one of the Sluts rolled over in his sleep and fell through a hole in the ceiling onto the next floor – and there wasn't even a lawsuit, he actually continued working on the film with his leg in a cast!) It was maverick, smash-and-grab filmmaking and it was marvellous fun.

*Opposite:* **Basil Pascali (Ben Kingsley) takes time out from spying**

**Ingrid (Frances McDormand) on the set of *Hidden Agenda***

*Below:* **Ken Loach (centre) and his crew**
The James Connolly club with a mural depicting a scene from the Republican struggle. Penny Eyles, continuity, sits behind the camera, Clive Tickner, the cameraman is smiling wryly as the director waves a vague hand towards the unseen actors.
**– Ken Loach, Director**

# FRANCES McDORMAND
## Actress, *Hidden Agenda*

I first met Mr Fellner in 1989 when he was producing Ken Loach's film *Hidden Agenda*. I never really knew why or how they found me since Ken had imagined the character of Ingrid as a German, but such are the mysteries of film financing. I was in LA working with Liam Neeson on Sam Raimi's *Darkman*. We were doing a lot of 'blue screen' work at the time and I was feeling dissatisfied with how technical my job had become.

I read Ken's script, not really understanding the full weight of its political implications and not knowing any of Ken's previous films. At work one day, I asked Liam if he knew a director named Ken Loach. He practically genuflected and breathlessly said, 'Do anything you must to meet and then work with the man!'. So on this extraordinary recommendation I agreed to pick up Ken at the hotel he was staying in (Ken walks when in LA!) and drive him to meet Eric at a house he was renting somewhere in the hills. When Ken got into the rental car the seatbelt automatically went around him and he cried out, 'That's awfully fascist wouldn't you say?' and I knew our meeting was going to be an interesting one. We spent the afternoon talking politics – humanistic and Irish – and I was caught in his spell. Thus I began a journey through the complicated world of a Ken Loach film.

# KEN LOACH
Director, *Hidden Agenda*

When David Puttnam was briefly at Columbia Pictures he rang me to see if I would be interested in making a film about the inquiry by the policeman John Stalker into the British shoot-to-kill policy in Ireland. Jim Allen wrote a script that encompassed not only the dirty war against Irish Republicans but also the conspiracy by mavericks in the Intelligence service – spies – to bring down the Wilson government. Heady stuff. Unfortunately David Puttnam left Columbia and we were left with Jim's script.

Coincidentally I had been working with Rebecca O'Brien at Working Title on a project that had failed to materialise. In the dog days that followed we thought we would try to find an executive producer for the Irish project. I think we stuck a pin in a list of independent production companies, not for witchcraft, but because we couldn't decide who to approach. Fortunately for us, we stabbed Eric.

So began the tortuous process of finding the money and making the film. Eric was supportive, enthusiastic and optimistic, good qualities when faced with a film that, as you would expect, got the cold shoulder from everyone here, TV and film alike. Eventually, a friend, Julia Kennedy, sat next to John Daly of Hemdale at a dinner party. The talk touched on our script. He was interested. Eric and John Daly struck a deal. The subtleties and nuances of their negotiations I can only guess at, but we were able to make the film.

As the script was hammered into shape the meetings between Jim Allen and Eric were memorable. A mutual, if unlikely, respect developed in Eric's gleaming, modern office that overlooked Golden Square, a respect that crossed boundaries of social standing and geography, as Jim's proletarian carrier bag sat incongruously on Eric's fine white carpet. Once, as we were waiting, Jim farted triumphantly on the leather sofa.

It was not an easy film to make. We had hoped to shoot the film in Belfast. The RUC were less than delighted and permissions were hard to come by. We tried Liverpool, which again proved difficult. Finally the interiors were mainly shot in north London and exteriors filmed on what purported to be 'recces' and 'rehearsals' in Belfast. One Loyalist parade was filmed for 'a documentary'.

Eric was always about to visit us in Belfast. We knew he was coming because he said so. Finally he made it on the last day. Unfortunately, because the unit had learned to be a moving target, he never caught up with us and went back home on the evening flight. Still, the thought was there. Maybe it was just as well. We had a rather heavy-handed visit from two RUC men who advised us to pack our bags.

The film had a lively reception at Cannes. It was attacked by a Tory MP as the 'IRA entry' and denounced by the Loyalist critic of the *Evening Standard* at the press conference, both signs of success, we thought. The jury gave it their Special Prize. Finally, as the Stevens Report has shown, we were right: there was collusion between the security forces and Loyalist terrorists.

**Jonathan Carlsson (Matt Dillon) kisses Ellen/Dorothy (Sean Young) in *A Kiss Before Dying***
I remember telling Matt [Dillon] that he was beautiful and he said, 'Don't call me beautiful. I'm a guy'. I always thought he was this really beautiful looking guy.
**– Sean Young, Actress**

*A Kiss Before Dying* will always remind me of a nervous journey from London to New York carrying huge and fragile balsa and plastic model of set, which is to fill 'H' Stage Shepperton. Sleepless night, anxious about presentation, complain twice about small, hot, smelly room – receptionist dismissive, unhelpful – 'That will be New York, Sir'. No appetite for breakfast, enter elevator for journey to meeting with Eric, James Dearden and Matt Dillon. Tiny elevator stops at fifth – doors open – David Hockney enters clutching large portfolio and squeezes in alongside huge model of set. 'Ow Do,' says David. Fellow Yorkshireman tones make me feel at home and I relax. We arrive at level one and meeting room. Shuffle out taking care with model and goodbyes to David. Elevator doors close smartish, crunching rear end of model. Heart sinks – all these miles and the last few yards! Fortunately trusty Art Directors Seagers and McLean have added balsa, UHU and scalpel knife to my hand luggage. (Couldn't travel so well equipped these days.) Hasty repairs outside meeting room and minutes later composure and model are restored to former glory. Enter meeting – Director abandons greetings, looks at model. 'Too small,' he says. 'Not half as small as it was ten minutes ago,' think I.
**– Jim Clay, Production Designer**

# JAMES DEARDEN
## Director, *A Kiss Before Dying*

After *Pascali's Island*, *A Kiss Before Dying* was an altogether different experience, not that it was horrible, but it seemed very serious by comparison. Serious because it was, for both Eric Fellner and myself, our first Studio project. Serious, because our budget was four times as great as we had for *Pascali* – a princely $12 million. Though the film was set in New York and Philadelphia, I had persuaded the studio and the US producer, Robert Lawrence, that we could shoot the bulk of the film at Shepperton and Pinewood, thus ensuring that I could renew my partnership with Eric, who would be the UK producer.

Cut to a suburban movie theatre in the Valley, some two years later, the first preview of the finished product. Eric and I are sitting with Robert Lawrence as the end credits roll. There have been some pretty awful test screenings, all sorts of rumours about 'problems' with the movie, and now we've even shot a new ending (which I'm told, but don't believe, means that the studio actually has confidence in the movie). But right now, at this moment, we're feeling pretty good, the new ending works, no one has walked out, and as far as we can judge the audience reaction is positive. As the lights come up, Tom Pollock, the head of the studio (and a man I have met only once before in my life) approaches, beaming. 'That was OK. I don't know what problems everyone's been talking about, but I really enjoyed it. You should see some of the stuff we put out!' He actually takes me by the arm and we walk together out of the auditorium into the foyer, like two lovers on a stroll. I'm walking on air.

Out in the foyer, Casey Silver, Head of Production, approaches, clutching bits of paper – the dreaded cards. He's frowning. Suddenly Tom is no longer at my side, he's in a huddle with Casey and the other executives. I catch the words 'cards' and 'brutal'. I glance over to Robert Lawrence, whose antennae are more finely tuned than mine in these matters. He's turned a deathly pale. Eric looks glum and distinctly nervous. I try to engage one of the lowlier executives, but am brushed aside. Suddenly I realize. We have become non-people. We have a highly communicable disease. We are the walking dead.

We slink off into the night. Out in the parking lot, Eric finally speaks. 'You suddenly realize how little power you have. This isn't England. It's a whole different ballgame. God, I never want to feel like that again.' I nod, but all I'm thinking is, 'WILL I EVER WORK AGAIN?'.

Eric learnt a fundamental lesson that night. Oh yes, and the name of the studio?
It was Universal.

**Cinematographer Mike Southon and Sean Young relax on the set of** *A Kiss Before Dying*

**Sean Young shares a joke with Camera Operator Philip Sindall and James Dearden (far right)**
Sean Young had been the subject of somewhat lurid press speculations concerning her behaviour on a previous film. It was also rumoured that I had based the bunny-boiling character in *Fatal Attraction* on her (completely untrue). So it was with some trepidation that I approached the filming of *A Kiss Before Dying*. As it turned out she was a model of good behaviour throughout and a joy to work with, as evidenced by this happy scene.
**– James Dearden, Director**

# 1990s

## THE POLYGRAM YEARS

EDWARD II
MAP OF THE HUMAN HEART
FOUR WEDDINGS AND A FUNERAL
THE HUDSUCKER PROXY
POSSE
PANTHER
ROMEO IS BLEEDING
MOONLIGHT AND VALENTINO
FRENCH KISS
DEAD MAN WALKING
FARGO
BEAN
THE BORROWERS
THE BIG LEBOWSKI
ELIZABETH
THE HI-LO COUNTRY
PLUNKETT & MACLEANE
NOTTING HILL

**Director Derek Jarman on the set of his 'Elizabethan Lay',** *Edward II*

# ON DEREK JARMAN

### From *Derek Jarman: a Biography* by Tony Peake

Aside from cracking a rather feeble joke that the introduction of as much sex and violence as the script could contain would help him achieve his aim of an 'Elizabethan Lay' rather than an 'Elizabethan Play', [Jarman] saw *Edward II* as one more skirmish in the battle he had joined on the pavement outside Bow Street. As an avowedly queer director, he wanted to make an unequivocally queer film.

Shooting started on Monday 18 February at Bray, near Windsor, in the old complex that had once been home to the Hammer House of Horror and was currently used both for film and as a recording studio. The building allotted to *Edward II* was as basic as the film's two sets, the steel-plated, semi-industrial prison and the series of black walls and cubes designed by Hobbs in such a way that they could be moved and rearranged to suggest an unlimited number of different spaces. The shoot lasted just five weeks and went like clockwork, with the satisfactory result that although it did not prove possible to film everything as scripted, the production did not overrun and, on Saturday 23 March, exactly on schedule, the words 'It's a wrap' were called, champagne was poured into plastic cups, and a 'beaming' Jarman was presented with 'a sturdily built, old-fashioned Raleigh Chiltern bicycle, complete with sensible wicker basket'.

After getting the job, the first time I visited the Working Title offices in Camden was for a rehearsal that Derek [Jarman] had called. A furious row was taking place between Derek and Ian McKellen over his knighthood. Derek thought he should turn it down in protest at the government's Clause 28. Which for a young actor on his first film, was an experience to see. It was a row being conducted over faxes so Derek was constructing the argument in front of us all.

**– Andrew Tiernan, Actor**

**Edward II (Steven Waddington, left) and Gaveston (Andrew Tiernan) embrace**

## LOUIS NOWRA
Writer, *Map of the Human Heart*

### 26 May 1991

Jeanne Moreau was on the set this morning having flown in from Paris last night. I had written the part of Sister Banville with her in mind. She refused Vincent [Ward, the director] at first but had not known just how stubborn he can be. He did not give up trying to woo her. There were flights to Paris, faxes, flowers and dinners until she gave in. Her voice is extraordinary. Deep and hoarse, the result of cigarettes, booze and God knows what else has been down her throat. In her early sixties she has a devastating coquettish smile. We talked about Australia as she has just been there doing a Wim Wenders movie. I wanted to ask her about working with Welles and Renoir, two of my favourite directors, but was too shy.

Vincent spent the morning on the scene in the cupboard where the two kids belt one another on the head with a stick and rolled up cardboard. There were takes after takes with Vincent yelling at the children as they hit each other. 'Hit him harder, Annie. No harder! Whack him! Harder!' until in one take she hit him so hard that she nearly knocked him out. Robert looked dazed and rubbed his head, wondering where he was. 'You think she's hitting him too hard?' I asked Vincent. A stupid question to put to a director. 'Course not,' he said, 'he can take it'.

A harassed-looking Tim Bevan arrived and his first words to me were, 'Have you made any cuts?'. I told him of the ones I had made and he grew nervous when I stopped. 'But you'll be cutting more, won't you?'. I lied and said, 'Of course', thinking I had cut all that I could. He grew edgy as the shoot went into overtime. 'You know, the butchers are coming,' he said between gritted teeth. After wrap was called I had drinks with Tim and I asked him who the butchers were. He was vague, calling them 'money men' who were 'nipping at his heel'. I am still unsure who the butchers are, but his tone of voice gave them a sinister aura.

**Young Albertine (Annie Gallipeau) and Young Avik (Robert Joamie) on the Montreal set of *Map of the Human Heart***
Both were a joy to work with and never once asked why an Australian screenwriter and New Zealand director wanted to tell a love story between a Metis (half breed) girl and an Inuit boy that ranged over fifteen years and went from the Canadian Arctic to the bombing of Dresden.
**– Louis Nowra, Writer**

I was walking past Jeanne's room when she called me in to have a chat. Her room has a religious icon on the wall and is packed with flowers. We were talking about some Australian actors we both knew when she leant across and whispered to me, 'Vincent is crazy, no?' I nodded my head vigorously. She brooded for a time and then turned back to me. 'Yes. I thought so. All the best directors are crazy.'

### 15 June 1991

Day of the exploding pigs. In this scene Avik and the German taxi driver head down a country road, discovering too late that it is mined. They avoid pigs, only to see the pigs step on the mines and explode. In the last mad days of the war, this is part of Avik's crazy journey out of Dresden.

Even before the first set up (the taxi driving down the hill in long shot) it began to rain heavily and didn't stop all day, turning the earth into muddy slush and making everyone's day miserable and exhausting. Vincent was the exception. These are the types of days when he comes alive, full of spirit and animation. It confirms his vision of the auteur against the elements. While the crew sought some kind of protection from the rain, he revelled in it. I hadn't seen him happier as when he stood in the cold, driving rain and giving orders through his megaphone. His broad grin gave him an uncomfortable resemblance to Hannibal Lecter. Steve, the completion guarantor, trying to stay dry in a yellow parka, stood in the muddy fields like some glum traffic cop. By late morning his Reeboks were unrecognizable. Vincent's *joie de vivre* in such trying circumstances unnerved him.

The morning was a grind, as the crew tried to get the fake pigs to explode in the proper way. I sought protection from the rain with a piece of plastic sheeting, but Tim Bevan, who arrived late, was beyond protection. I had never seen him so desperate. Jet lagged and jittery, he wandered the cold, rainy fields as one by one the pigs exploded. He wore a woollen jumper that as it became more sodden grew progressively longer, passing from just below his waist to near his knees. With his wet clothes, matted hair and bedraggled appearance, he resembled a madman from central casting. Obviously our money problems are greater than he is letting on. 'You know,' he said, 'they can still take the film from him.' Tim had to fly back to London and did not stay until the end of the day's shoot. He was driven away, sodden and depressed. I think his last words to me were, 'The butchers are coming', but it was hard to hear over the noise of another pig exploding.

*Left to right*: **Louis Nowra, Tim Bevan and Tim White in the ceiling of the Royal Albert Hall, on the set of *Map of the Human Heart***
The producers Tim Bevan (middle) and Tim White (right) pretend rapt interest in what the screenwriter, Louis Nowra, is saying. In a few hours' time, Nowra will find himself directing second unit downstairs while the director, Vincent Ward, will be risking life and limb by hanging from the ceiling, by only a rope, in order to get the final shot of the night.
**– Louis Nowra, Writer**

# VINCENT WARD
Director, *Map of the Human Heart*

### The Leap

I was struck mostly by the way Tim Bevan seemed to ignore obstacles. If there was a ravine in front of him whilst raising the finance, he would seem to leap over it, ignoring the details of the challenges shrieking up towards him so that he could deal with them on his own terms when ready. He focused only on the end game, keeping supportive throughout. This was especially difficult as his company was being purchased at the time, and there was some reluctance from PolyGram to proceed with this film as part of its slate. *Map of the Human Heart* had all the difficulties you would expect from making a film in three continents and filming in the Arctic (the least of which being a director getting frostbite during the lengthy preparation). Yet surprisingly this film experience was the one in which I felt most supported. For in making those leaps Tim would take you with him.

But there were funny, extreme moments too. The first time Tim visited the set was on the third to last day of filming. By then I was completely burnt out and humourless, especially since my father had died in New Zealand while we kept on filming in Canada. Now I stumbled into the catering bus that was parked outside the Albert Hall – our location for the day. I am afraid I wasn't as open to a producer at this late stage of production as perhaps one should be. We all sat down for breakfast of large plates of mushy eggs and baked beans: co-writer Louis Nowra, producer Tim Bevan and line producer Redmond Morris. Then Tim demanded shooting order adjustments. I stood up hastily from the table, jarring it and causing my plate of runny eggs and gelatinous beans to bounce (some of which partially splattered on Tim's face) and left them to dine alone. I swear this was an accident. Wiping the detritus from his face, Tim announced with typical elan, 'Well, I guess that showed him'. Louis Nowra, his irony barely covert, agreed with him.

By the end of the day Tim had allowed me to proceed with stunt camera work myself, above the inner dome of the Albert Hall, a hundred odd metres above the ground-floor seating. There was no one else available to do this task so I volunteered. But in a sense we both took the leap. Those who knew me least looked worried, but Tim kept a broad, almost benign expression across his face and as I lost my balance, then swung from the

ceiling and hurtled out of control for a central iron girder, I wondered if Tim, in a private moment, darkly humourous, may have thought this appropriate solace for the baked beans of that morning. The camera collided with the girder and I went aerobically on a tail-spin into the decking. And nothing more was said… Just that very wry smile on seeing that I was OK.

**Map of the Human Heart**
**director Vincent Ward discusses**
**a scene with his leading actress**
**Anne Parillaud on location in**
**the Royal Albert Hall**

*Opposite:* **Young Avik (Robert Joamie) is bounced high in the air by his fellow Inuits**

# BILLY HINSHELWOOD
Lawyer

After the resurgence in the second half of the 1980s of the independent British film the landscape had begun to look a little familiar by the beginning of the 1990s. These films for the most part had been relatively low budget and generally set in the UK and the American marketplace was becoming more circumspect about buying them.

It was time in 1990 to break the mould, to produce bigger-budget films with more international scope. When Vincent Ward approached Working Title with the screenplay for *Map Of The Human Heart*, it was clear the film's budget would be considerably higher than the usual Working Title model. Logistically the film was not easy as a number of scenes needed genuine ice and snow for the Arctic sequences. The casting came together with a distinctly international flavour, Anne Parillaud (Luc Besson's original *Nikita*), John Cusack playing an extended cameo, Jeanne Moreau, Jason Scott Lee (then an unknown) and Patrick Bergin. All that was then needed was the money.

Much is written today about the accessing of soft funds and co-production monies and about the intricacy of the structures involved. Yet I suspect few of today's films could match the structural complexity of *Map*. Co-producers from four countries – France, England, Canada and Australia – accessed two separate co-production treaties. Japanese equity finance came into the mix together with an American pre-sale to Miramax. All of this had to be accommodated within an overall German tax structure and the requirements of a Dutch lending bank. The lawyers were kept busy.

But so was the producer. Tim Bevan faced an arduous and difficult schedule and a very tight budget. Anything that could have gone wrong in the snow did. Cranes collapsed down glaciers. An irate and exhausted director threw his breakfast at his harassed producer when he was refused overtime for an extended shoot in the ice. But after an extremely tough time the shoot was finally completed and it included a number of quite magnificent scenes, including the star-crossed protagonists making love on the top of a barrage balloon.

After an extended post-production period, the film was finished and delivered. It was not a huge success commercially, but it represented a considerable watershed and step forward in the kind of film that Working Title, in particular, and the UK film industry in general, was producing. It showed above all what could be achieved in terms of scope and ambition with a huge amount of perseverance and sheer bloody-mindedness.

**Love is in the air: Setting up the scene for Avik and Albertine's illicit moment of passion atop a wartime barrage balloon in *Map of the Human Heart***

# TIM WHITE
## Producer, *Map of the Human Heart*

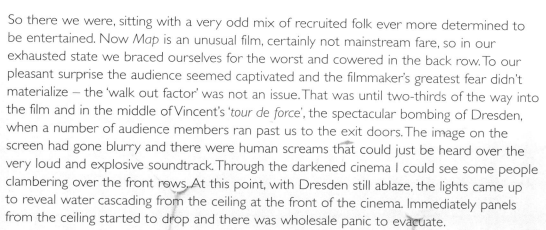

One incident towards the end of the making of *Map of the Human Heart* epitomized the journey of the film. It was mid-winter in New Jersey and the film's North American distributor, Miramax, had arranged an audience test screening. Vincent and I had flown the excruciating twenty-two hours from Sydney with the double-head print. During the tech set-up there were some disconcerting signs that all would not go to plan. By the time the recruited audience started to show up to the suburban multiplex there was four inches of snow outside. Inside we were increasingly agitated because the sound and picture would not interlock. Thirty minutes or so after the scheduled screening time we had to turn the cold and frustrated audience away and request they return an hour later. The Miramax recruiters assured us the inevitable 'no shows' would be replaced by audiences from other films in the multiplex. By the time we were ready to roll two hours late the only film spilling out was *Wayne's World*.

So there we were, sitting with a very odd mix of recruited folk ever more determined to be entertained. Now *Map* is an unusual film, certainly not mainstream fare, so in our exhausted state we braced ourselves for the worst and cowered in the back row. To our pleasant surprise the audience seemed captivated and the filmmaker's greatest fear didn't materialize – the 'walk out factor' was not an issue. That was until two-thirds of the way into the film and in the middle of Vincent's '*tour de force*', the spectacular bombing of Dresden, when a number of audience members ran past us to the exit doors. The image on the screen had gone blurry and there were human screams that could just be heard over the very loud and explosive soundtrack. Through the darkened cinema I could see some people clambering over the front rows. At this point, with Dresden still ablaze, the lights came up to reveal water cascading from the ceiling at the front of the cinema. Immediately panels from the ceiling started to drop and there was wholesale panic to evacuate.

Standing in the foyer, with a supportive but enraged Harvey Weinstein screaming for answers, one of the multiplex staff sheepishly approached to explain that there had been a blockage in the plumbing in the women's toilets. Just what spilled onto that audience doesn't bear thinking about.

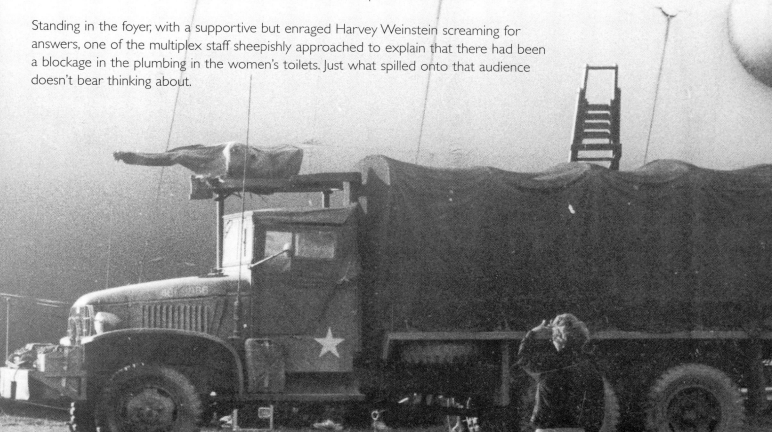

## WENDY PALMER
President Manifesto Film Sales 1990–92

When I left Handmade Films in 1988 after nine years as Director of Marketing and Distribution, I had the germ of an idea. I had observed that the output of a production company can vary tremendously year to year – in a good year perhaps five films, in a bad year, perhaps not even one. This was disastrous for a film sales company, so why not form a sales company that was selling films for more than one producer/production company, thus hopefully allowing for the vagaries of development and production timing?

Two British production companies sprang to mind immediately – Initial Films and Working Title. Young, aggressive and cutting edge, both had neither an established relationship with a sales company, nor easy access to finance from presales to foreign distributors. First stop was to see my old friend Eric Fellner. He immediately saw the interest in my idea and was definitely in, subject to all the obvious caveats. Working Title's Tim Bevan, was keen but a little more hesitant. Promising to provide a business plan if he came back with serious interest, I awaited his discussions and subsequent meetings with his then partners. I immersed myself in each company's considerable development slate.

My balloon burst a little the day Tim phoned me and said he did not think my idea worked with Eric and Initial. His reasoning was that the product of Initial and Working Title was too similar and that the sales company slate and thus the production companies would benefit more from an American partner, providing those all-important sexier US stars. I was on the horns of a dilemma. I knew Tim was right, but then who did I go with? Tim or Eric? Tricky. In the end I decided that the decision had to be based on the script and development material they had provided me with – it's much easier to sell something you like. It was a hard call and there followed a painful conversation with Eric, which I would much rather forget, if it wasn't for the irony of the delightful success of their latter partnership.

And so began, with Tim, Sarah and Graham, a long search for our perfect American partner. Time passed and eventually the inevitable happened and I took other means to pay the bills. Some months later I bumped into Tim in LA. Tim had met a guy called Michael Kuhn at PolyGram who had an investment in a very groovy LA video and film production company called Propaganda, and PolyGram's backing to proceed, cautiously, into film production.

Within four months Manifesto Film Sales was launched with three staff – John Durie, Caroline Burton and myself – and two films on its slate – Working Title's *Chicago Joe and the Showgirl* and Propaganda's *Wild at Heart*. I spent the next three years on the most exhilarating rollercoaster ride of my career.

## PAUL WEBSTER
### Working Title Films 1988–93

After-work gatherings in the George pub on Wardour Street in the late 1980s. Tim, Michael Kuhn and Graham Bradstreet plotting the rise of PolyGram. Graham explaining to me the nature of German tax-based financing, me nodding along, not understanding a word. Nik Powell saying to Tim over a pint: 'I can't understand you Tim, why do you want to run a big company well when you can be like me and run a small one badly'. Guffaws all round.

1990. Off to Los Angeles to produce *Drop Dead Fred* and start up Working Title LA. Clarissa Troop and I shared a house which doubled as the office. Bossing Clarissa around all day only to have the tables turned as evening came, finding myself doing exactly what I was told as the cocktails came out and we prepared for the evening's entertainment.

Back in London, Richard is writing a new script, something about weddings and funerals. I read a draft, we talk about it, 'Are you going to produce it, Paulie?' 'Well, no, probably not, I've got to do *Romeo Is Bleeding* in New York'. On such conversations careers change. Oh well.

**Young Avik (Robert Joamie), the boy Inuit in *Map of the Human Heart***

**Tim Robbins shelters from the rain between takes on the set of one of Bob Roberts's political pop videos.** *Bob Roberts* **was Working Title's first collaboration with Tim Robbins, who both starred in and directed this 1992 feature**

In 1990, I had moved to Los Angeles and was asked to set up the US office of Working Title at 2017 Taft Avenue. During our time in the house, Working Title came under PolyGram's banner. There were daily messages from someone called 'Kuhn' who at the time I had no idea was to become very important in Working Title's life and also a good friend. Paul was busy setting up *Drop Dead Fred* and *Rubin & Ed*. All in all it was a rather wonderful but strange time, and I was very sorry when we finally gave up the house and moved to the A&M lot.
**– Clarissa Troop,
Working Title Films**

# MICHAEL KUHN
### President, PolyGram Filmed Entertainment

'Fuck, fuck, fuck, fuck…' Hugh Grant said this quite a lot at the beginning of *Four Weddings and a Funeral*. Tim, Eric and I said it quite a lot in the early years of Working Title and PolyGram. Before Eric appeared on the scene, Tim and I said nothing else for several years.

We learned together. Early disappointments (*For Queen and Country*, *Diamond Skulls*, *Fools of Fortune*, *London Kills Me*, *Map of the Human Heart*) taught us many important lessons: spend tons of money on development and don't expect scripts to happen in less than five years; the power of marketing and distribution is tremendously important; we *can* make films that compete in the world market.

In the early years, I saved their butts by ensuring that no failure or string of failures was financially bad enough to sink them. In later years they saved my butt with some big commercial and critical hits – *Four Weddings and a Funeral*, *Bean*, *Elizabeth*, *Fargo*, *Bob Roberts* and many others.

*Miscellaneous Memories:*
When at Livonia Street, Working Title shared offices with Manifesto Films, our sales company. As a result no-one was sober after 4p.m. on any day of the week… When at Water Lane, Camden, dead bodies were found in the canal it overlooked, with such regularity no one remarked on it.

Eric is the best schmoozer. Tim is crap at it and I come in a poor second. Tim, however, has the lowest tolerance for bullshit. I am second. Eric, knowing it's bullshit, can put up with it for the longest time if required. I taught them how to be grumpy and perfect a sulk so people could feel it twenty yards away.

The rest of those ten years is a blank. We are still friends.

# STEWART TILL
President of International, PolyGram Filmed Entertainment

When I joined PolyGram Filmed Entertainment, in January 1992, Working Title had made more than their fair share of under-performing films. They were financially haphazard, with Companies House consistently threatening legal action for non-filing of year-end accounts.

In the nineties, if you had to describe Working Title, you would talk about a company with fiercely loyal, long-serving staff, producers that understood and were comfortable in both London and Los Angeles, a company run by two headstrong partners who did not tolerate fools, who respected and delegated to expertise when they found it and who had an instinctive ability to discover the sharpest writing and directing talents, people who then remained loyal to the company, sometimes film after film. You would inevitably mention a scruffy dress sense, expensive cars, aversion to paperwork, Richard Curtis, constant trans-Atlantic travel, films with a British sensibility but a worldwide audience, very popular Christmas parties and overpowering flattering press coverage.

Back then, Working Title was unrecognizable as the company that, at least for the last five years, has single-handedly achieved success for the British film industry in the worldwide market place. Also, it is probably fair to say that Working Title bore little resemblance to the company that has produced well over a billion dollars of box office and gathered BAFTAs, Oscars® and Césars too many to count.

Yet, even back then, ten years ago, Working Title had the sort of values they have today, and stood for the same business and creative filmmaking principles they consistently live by today.

*Left to right:* **Eric Fellner, Tim Bevan and Stewart Till launching** *French Kiss* **at the Cannes Film Festival, May 1994**

*Left to right:* **PFE's Success Story: Promotional artwork for** *Bean,* ***The Borrowers, Fargo*** **and** *Elizabeth*

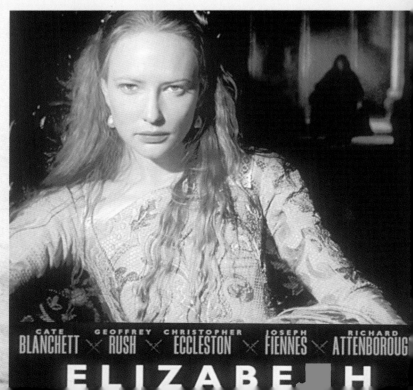

CATE **BLANCHETT** × GEOFFREY **RUSH** × CHRISTOPHER **ECCLESTON** × JOSEPH **FIENNES** × RICHARD **ATTENBOROUG**

# ELIZABE H

## ANTHONY JONES
Agent, Peters Fraser & Dunlop

### A Fairy Story

Once upon a time, a young English screenwriter wrote an original romantic comedy.

His agent looked on it and saw that it was good and sold a short option to an equally young but impoverished independent production company still more or less struggling to keep its head above water. And they had a director and a promising cast and scrabbled to get the money together. And they just about did. The film was made and indeed released to modest acclaim in the UK and the rest of the world, but not in America. And no more was thought about it either artistically or financially.

But about nine months later, the production company, much to its surprise, received an unexpected windfall in the shape of a cheque from one of the television companies with whom they had set the film up. They hadn't been expecting it, and indeed, their finances were in such a parlous position that they needed every penny they could find. When they looked at the accounting of the film they saw that the arrival of this cheque would, remarkably enough, put the film into profit and that if it did so, they would have to pay out an unexpectedly large cheque both to the writer and director of the film. They also knew that, under the sophisticated and dubious practices which go under the name of 'net profit accounting', they could bury this cheque in the system and no one would be any the wiser. But, for once, their baser instincts were suppressed and they sent out the profit cheques – much to the surprise of the agent, writer, director and indeed other recipients who had not been expecting anything at all. So everyone said thank you.

And then it came to pass that twelve months later the self-same writer wrote another original screenplay, and he went to his agent and said, 'To whom shall we offer this masterpiece – we have the world to choose from'. And they said to themselves, 'Well, these producers do at least seem to be honest,' (having by now sent a second cheque) 'so let's give them another go'.

And they did.

And thus it was that Working Title received a first draft of *Four Weddings and a Funeral*.

So, just for once in the film business, virtue was rewarded.

**Mike Newell (right) explains a scene to Anna Chancellor and Hugh Grant in *Four Weddings and a Funeral***

It all looks very tense. We had thirty-seven days to make the film so it probably was very tense. Nobody suspected what would happen. Duncan Kenworthy and Richard Curtis were full of bounce and optimism as we took the film to California for its first preview. Me, Eeyore as always, predicted ritual humiliation. The audience laughed within the first twenty seconds and didn't stop until the end. So much for prediction.
**– Mike Newell, Director**

'You're not being funny any more, it's turning into a Lorca play.' Mike to us.
**– Anna Chancellor, Actress**

I had not laughed as uncontrollably whilst reading anything until the script of *Four Weddings and a Funeral* was sent to me. It transpired that neither had anyone else. It soon became the film everyone was dying to be part of. For the leading role Hugh Grant was discussed straight away and, although we went ahead and met most of his contemporaries, he remained the front runner. He possessed all the 'matinée idol' qualities required for the role, with the added bonus of a large dose of humour. When it came to the 'friends', we gathered together a fairly disparate group of actors who were all memorably hilarious and moving in their playing of a 'fairly disparate group of characters'. A generous Simon Callow hooted helplessly with laughter at the read-through, only once his character had suffered his demise of course.
**– Michelle Guish, Casting Director**

**Fiona (Kristin Scott Thomas) and Charles (Hugh Grant) at Angus and Laura's wedding in *Four Weddings and a Funeral***

# RICHARD CURTIS
Writer, *Four Weddings and a Funeral*

### Are your films autobiographical?
Only in the sense that they're about things I might have done. All my films seem to start with autobiographical romantic moments that I never had the nerve to actually do anything about. I never asked the nurse who turned up as Emma Thompson's character in *The Tall Guy* on a date – and *Four Weddings* is based on an incident when I danced with a gorgeous girl at a wedding, who asked me where I was staying that night. I was in fact staying at the same hotel as her but I told her that I had just agreed to go home with my friends, which I did – and I never saw her again.

### What about the rest of *Four Weddings* – is it taken from life?
Well, at one point, I went to seventy-two weddings in five years and a lot of the things that happened in that movie actually happened – but the structure just popped into my head one day, although it was originally *Four Weddings and a Honeymoon*. When I explained the plot to my friend Helen Fielding, I could tell she despised the 'Honeymoon' bit, which I envisaged à la Dudley Moore/Bo Derek beach sequence in *10*. So we decided we'd have a go at being more serious. The incident which inspired the funeral had actually taken place at a wedding I attended – a man standing next to me had a heart attack during the best man's speech – although, happily, he didn't die.

### Was it easy to get the film from script to screen?
*Four Weddings and a Funeral* had a much harder birth than *The Tall Guy*, because we were just above that line financially where things start to matter. And it never felt particularly like a hit. When I had handed the script in to Tim he probably thought, as did we all, 'Here's another one like the last one, let's hope it does a little bit better than *The Tall Guy*'.

### When did Mike Newell come on board?
Once we had finished the screenplay, Emma Freud (who was by this stage script editing) and I took the directorial decision very seriously – the script had seemingly taken us a lifetime to write, so we wanted the right person for the job. We sat at home and spent three weeks just watching films – until we happened on a Jack Rosenthal TV film called *Ready When You Are, Mr McGill* which Mike had directed ten years earlier – and felt we had found our man.

### Why?
Mike just seemed able to capture the basic truthfulness of quite big comic characters with an almost documentary realism. He seemed ideal to take my light entertainment script and make it something more than its parts. And thank God, Tim once again let us have our choice.

### And how did Duncan Kenworthy get involved?
Paul Webster wasn't available, he was working on *Romeo is Bleeding* in America. I didn't know Duncan very well, but what I did know was that he had a very classy and tasteful eye – the things he'd produced were beautiful – and he cared passionately about the projects he worked on – I thought he'd make sure it didn't feel like a television film.

### So how did you get your cast together?

Mike was rather obsessive about casting. You would have these bizarre occasions when someone would come in to play a one-line vicar – and Mike would turn to me and say, 'So Richard, tell us about the vicar'. And I'd say, 'Well, he says "I now declare you man and wife"'. And Mike would say, 'No, no, no – I mean, how long has he been working in the church and what's his attitude to marriage?' He wanted 360 degrees of every character – which meant that by the time we shot the film, not only had it been perfectly cast, but the actors had been in to see us three times – so they really knew their parts, and all of us knew all about the characters. It was a fantastic bit of methodology and I think added real depth to some very shallow things.

### What happened with Hugh?

The key thing I have learned is that the central characters of my films tend to be slightly dull. Because they are surrounded by more exotic characters, they have to be truthful and normal. But the difficulty is to make that slightly dull character interesting. Hugh was the first person to show us that he could capture the potential funniness in the character.

*Left to right:* **The Magnificent Seven: Fiona (Kristin Scott Thomas), Charles (Hugh Grant), Gareth (Simon Callow), Carrie (Andie MacDowell), Scarlett (Charlotte Coleman), Matthew (John Hannah) and Tom (James Fleet) all pose for the camera**

## What was it like working with him?

Fun. He was very, very self-deprecating in those days. In fact it was difficult to see through the self-mockery to the quality of the performance that he was actually giving. He had this joke about the fact that he could only do three types of acting: 1) normal, 2) sexy – by dropping his voice an octave, and 3) serious – by raising his voice an octave. When shooting the scene with James Fleet just after the funeral, he said, 'Today's a chipmunk day', and sure enough if you listen, his voice is distinctly higher in that scene than elsewhere in the film. I don't think I saw at the time what he was actually achieving – which was playing his part perfectly, and becoming my definitive romantic hero.

## Did the film turn out as you hoped?

I feel Mike directed the film completely flawlessly. On the subject of truth in my films, it was a real education. It's what I have aspired to and worked towards since then. I think it's the only one of my films that was very nearly right straight away – it had been such a short shoot, thirty-six days and there had been no time for mistakes, and Mike didn't make any. He and Duncan did a quality job.

## How did the testing of the film go?

The film seemed to be going down well in the UK but our expectations for the US were zero. PolyGram had it marked down to earn $0 in the States. We all thought it would be a similar experience to *The Tall Guy*. But when we took the film to Santa Monica, it in fact scored higher than it had done in the UK. I've never quite understood what the difference was – but the strange thing is that ever since then our films have tested the same in both countries. Though I have to say, even after the test, we weren't confident. I remember when we were asked to open the Sundance Festival, Mike was keen to send the film quickly, because he was convinced the festival didn't know what it was getting – 'I don't want them ending up with a "pig in a poke"', he said.

## So you were surprised by the American success?

Yes. Our biggest dream was to make more than Mike's last film, *Enchanted April*, which had made $12 million. And it could easily have ended up around there had not Working Title and PolyGram got the bit between their teeth. I remember being with Michael Kuhn when he got a call with the American figures for the first week. He had to make a snap decision whether to spend $15 million to widen the release from the small number of screens it was showing on to a thousand screens across the country. It seemed surreal to us, not having been able to find even $4 million to make the movie, that in one phone call they should spend four times the cost of the film in Prints and Advertising – a truly lateral leap of faith to spend that amount of money on something that had cost so little to make.

*Opposite:* **Carrie (Andie MacDowell) and Charles (Hugh Grant) on the set of *Four Weddings and a Funeral*, with Director Mike Newell in the background**

*Four Weddings and a Funeral* was a real opportunity for character costume design and comedy, with the added challenge of needing to make each wedding look different. It also had fantastic characterful actors, with Andie MacDowell and Hugh Grant to play with. Joy. Well, not quite… all those sunny weddings, where everyone was meant to look radiant and warm, were actually freezing and wet in reality, and the poor wardrobe workers struggled to keep it all from becoming sodden and drooping. Also, the morning line-up to dish out hats for the extras, was something to behold… the rest is history. I think Richard Curtis is a genius at reflecting the preoccupations of our times.
**– Lindy Hemming, Costume Designer**

*Opposite:* **Duckface (Anna Chancellor) punches Charles (Hugh Grant) at the altar as Matthew (John Hannah) looks on**
Hugh was wearing a little skull cap, kirby-gripped onto his hair, in case he fell. 'Please don't hurt me Anna, I can tell you're violent.'
**– Anna Chancellor, Actress**

# DUNCAN KENWORTHY
Producer, *Four Weddings and a Funeral*

In a way, the Oscars® helped us even with *Four Weddings*. When Mike Newell and I were sent to LA in March 1993 to cast the part of Carrie (eventually played by Andie MacDowell), we went proffering Richard 'Noël Coward' Curtis's witty script but a distinctly meagre paycheque – not usually the best of combinations to attract top-flight American talent. By a lucky accident we were there just as *Enchanted April* got two Best Supporting Actress nominations, and every young Hollywood actress wanted to be in a low-budget movie directed by Mike Newell.

Since there were just the two of us (Richard couldn't make it and has never forgiven me), I ended up reading the part of Charles in all the auditions. Mike, of course, had to watch the actresses at work. If you've seen the film, you'll know that the only bits that highlight Carrie's role are the love scenes with Charles. So I can claim to have 'skulked around' at the Jolly Boatman hotel exchanging kisses with sixteen of Hollywood's most beautiful and talented young actresses. For most of these there was a conference table between us and the kisses were mimed. But on the happy day when the conference room was unavailable, I was heavily smooched by a beautiful and famous young actress whose actor husband, she later told us, was away on location. She may have been shortsighted, but she nearly got the part.

**Charlotte Coleman (left), Duncan Kenworthy and Kristin Scott Thomas relax between takes**

Charlotte's trying to make me laugh, but Kristin's clearly hot and bothered at being in my presence – and finding it hard to compose herself. Must be my Comme des Garcons jacket. I'm trying to affect an 'I can't help being so attractive' sort of look. I can't think why our stills photographer, Stephen Morley, wanted me in the shot – taken on an Edwardian sofa in the drafty hallway of the Old House at Shepperton Studios – but he's been in my good books ever since.
– Duncan Kenworthy, Producer

# MICHAEL FOSTER
Agent

In January 1994 after I had attended various successful audience screenings in the UK of *Four Weddings and a Funeral*, I travelled with Hugh Grant to the snowy peaks of Park City, Utah, where *Four Weddings* had been invited to open the Sundance Film Festival. PolyGram was feeling very up, excited and hopeful for this beautifully made film that Mike Newell and Duncan Kenworthy, Tim and Eric had fashioned from Richard Curtis's second screenplay. Hugh and Mike did lots of press for a day or so and understatedly said that they hoped the film would please its public and would give Working Title a successful, well-received British picture.

The picture was to premiere in a 1,300-seat theatre in downtown Salt Lake City, the centre of Mormon culture and, we were told, a very conservative city. After a glitzy opening reception the hordes piled into the auditorium, not a seat to be had anywhere. A few pleasant speeches followed and, as the lights went down, Hugh and I retired to stand at the back of the theatre. We prepared to bask in the triumph of hearing the audience revel in the glory of Hugh's rendition of Richard's script. Never has an agent felt so much nachas.

The first lines of the film that are uttered, as our hero wakes to the sound of his alarm clock and then wakes up the most wonderful Charlotte Coleman, were that day forever burnt onto my memory:

'O, Fuck
       Fuck
          O, Fuck
             Fuck, Fuck, Fuck, Fuck, Fuck,

Fuck it,

Well, Fuck me!'.

With every further expletive all we could hear from the audience was not the roar of their laughter but the continued
          thwack
            thwack
              thwack
                thwack
                  thwack!

of literally hundreds of seats flinging back as the disgusted burghers of Salt Lake City stampeded for the exits in stony shuffling silence. By the time this sea of people had pushed past Hugh and myself, the auditorium was barely two-thirds full and we knew that despite our sides having split with laughter at these scenes of devastated Mormon migration, this was one movie that was definitely not going to play in Peoria and would not bring Working Title the commercial success for which it had so long craved.

Duncan Kenworthy offered me the job on *Four Weddings* despite Jane Frazer not wanting me because I was 'scarily quiet' (I suspect that no-one else was available). Working on that film was very special – it's the most fun I have ever had on any film. The joy was that by the time we, the crew, all joined, Mike Newell, Duncan, Richard Curtis and Working Title had completely figured out the film they wanted to make. The first time I met Mike Newell he said, 'Darling, I'm sure you have already heard that I screamed all the way through my last film'. In fact, he never took his frustration out on anyone – the only casualty we had was one set of headphones which he would sometimes rip off his head and throw to the ground. He was so aware of our financial constraints that he made sure that each department only invested their budget in areas that he wanted. We couldn't afford to give Hugh Grant any kind of dressing room – he never complained, but half-way through, Duncan took pity on him and we gave him the cheapest, smallest English caravan, complete with curly lino on the floor. I know the whole crew look back on the experience of *Four Weddings* with huge affection – there was such a feeling of unity and fun, despite the low salaries. And then, once the film was hugely successful, Working Title very kindly sent a cheque to every single person who had been involved in it as a 'thank you'.

**– Mary Richards, Line Producer**

**Shooting the Teaser Trailer: Carrie (Andie MacDowell) and Charles (Hugh Grant) play up to the camera in this promotional trailer for *Four Weddings and a Funeral***

## ALAN PELL
### Deputy Head of A&R for Mercury Records 1987–2001

At the tail end of 1993, I received a call from Roger Ames, Chairman of the PolyGram Music Group, asking me to work with Working Title to put together a soundtrack for *Four Weddings and a Funeral*. I was told the time frame was quite tight for this, however I was confident this would represent no problem at all.

It turned out to be quite a big problem. I watched the nearly finished film and had my first meeting with Richard Curtis and Duncan Kenworthy. Slowly the magnitude of this job, which I had taken on without any idea of the substantially different working practices of the film world, started to dawn. As it was nearly Christmas, access to major artists willing to record at short notice presented the first major problem.

Nightmare followed nightmare, and although the trials and tribulations of the next few months would make a book themselves (albeit a fairly dull one, unless endless phone calls and contract law are your thing), slowly deadlines were met, songs were recorded, videos were shot and finally, a couple of weeks prior to the movie's launch, Wet Wet Wet's version of the old Troggs hit 'Love Is All Around' was finally released. It spent fifteen weeks at number one and became one of the most successful single releases of all time. The soundtrack album fared extremely well and as the film was rolled out around the world played a major part in helping it to become a record-breaking success.

*Four Weddings* holds a special place in my heart and I am immensely proud of my contribution to what was to become a fantastic and uniquely British worldwide phenomenon.

The film opened in the US in early March of 1994, and even though it was a 'platform release' – which meant theatres were slowly added every week around the country – the initial screen grosses kept going up at the box office from week to week, rather than going down the usual twenty-five to fifty per cent, which would have been our expectations as the film widened out. All of this was topped when the film reached the number one position in the US box office on its fifth weekend. This film taught me much about vision and chemistry – Richard Curtis and Mike Newell were indeed great chemistry and I certainly haven't seen the linking of a great writer and director quite like this since.
**– Russell Schwartz, President, Gramercy Pictures 1992-99**

# JULIETTE DOW
## Assistant to Tim Bevan 1990–2000

**7 May 1994:** It is the day after the UK premiere of *Four Weddings and a Funeral*, and Natascha Wharton and I (then assistants to Eric Fellner and Tim Bevan respectively) are en route to the Cannes Film Festival. Nursing hangovers we pore over pictures of Elizabeth Hurley in 'that dress' – a star is indeed born. We have tickets to *The Hudsucker Proxy* that night and a room at the Carlton. Too good to be true? Oh yes, dear readers, it was…

**6.00p.m.** A distressed Kieran Breen from PolyGram has a problem: Mr Grant and Miss Hurley are tonight's guests of honour, BA have lost Hugh's luggage, he's had to buy emergency clothes at Nice airport and they don't have time to go via the Hotel du Cap to change. Can they use our room for half an hour? Ever willing to oblige we agree and prepare to move out.

**6.15.** No time – the 'couple du jour' are suddenly in our room. We try to leave but wires are crossed – they assume we are staff of some sort but there is no time for explanation. Hugh disappears into the shower, requesting an iron, and Elizabeth needs footwear as her shoes were in Hugh's lost bag. With a cry of 'I'll wear anything from a size five to a size seven' we race up to the PolyGram cocktail party to see if anyone can save the day.

**6.30.** Mission accomplished, we return to the fray. Elizabeth is in the shower, and no sign of room service. Hugh's trousers are too short so I hastily take down the hems – minus iron they look passable. Elizabeth steps into her dress. A floaty Versace creation split to the thigh – she looks fantastic. 'Got a needle and thread?' Ever the Girl Guide I have and without further ado, Elizabeth lifts her 'embonpoint' into its rightful position with one hand, pulls in the dress at the back and directs me to sew it – I do as I'm told. Finally they are both ready.

**6.45.** A whirlwind has passed through our room. We are too late to go to the screening now so we collapse and watch all the red carpet action on TV instead. We both need a drink!

**7.15.** They're back. They've posed for their photo call, but on finding their seats occupied have decided to have a romantic dinner instead. They change, re-pack their bags and finally we get the chance to explain who we are. Lots of thank yous and apologies – 'Sorry to disturb', as Charles from *Four Weddings* would have put it.

We fly home nursing new hangovers, and thankfully the latest photos of 'Leeez and OOOuug' show no evidence of my sewing skills… So, not quite the Cannes experience we were expecting, but definitely a true example of the madness we love that is the film industry.

**Ethan Coen (left), Tim Robbins (centre), Anna Nicole Smith and Joel Coen**

On the set of *The Hudsucker Proxy* Joel Coen explains the physics of the yo-yo to Tim Robbins while Ethan Coen, aware of being upstaged, winks at Anna Nicole Smith. She later sued him for sexual harassment.

**– Ethan Coen, Filmmaker**

## JOEL AND ETHAN COEN
Filmmakers

### A Reminiscence

I first remember meeting Eric in the lobby of the Carlton Hotel in Cannes. I was introduced to him briefly by the Coen Brothers. It was most unmemorable, Eric doesn't grab you at first, and I just thought he was another Brit trying to get a couple of independent films made. Some months later I found, to my surprise, that he had stayed in touch with the Coens and they'd decided that they were going to make an overall deal with him, as Eric had become part of PolyGram. I said, 'Really, you like this guy that much, huh?'. And they said, 'Yeah, we like Eric. He's not very pushy, and we think he gets what we're doing'. And then I said, 'Well, let me get to know him a little bit and we'll try to work something out'.
**– Jim Berkus, Agent for the Coen Brothers, United Talent Agency**

We were hard at work promoting one of our movies for Working Title at the Cannes Film Festival a few years ago. Our days were a dreary routine of early rising, serial and punishingly repetitive press interviews through the morning, a hurried lunch, and then more punishingly repetitive press interviews until a dinner that usually involved being interviewed once again by press of various nations who rotated with each course. After dinner some quasi-social function would be scheduled that was in fact further promotion, usually among distributors whose territories ranged from the middling to the microscopic. The conversation, sadly, was generally a reprise of the interviews we'd given during the day, only now we were allowed to hold a glass of white wine. This was meant to suggest that the occasion was indeed social, but the wine, combined with the grinding conversation, only acted as a soporific and by the time our minders released us we had only enough energy left to stumble bleary-eyed to bed. Six hours later we would be roused and the routine would begin again.

Occasionally Eric Fellner would cheerfully 'pop in' to offer a few words of encouragement and then hurry off to tend to his own busy schedule. One time, however, he forgot his date book and we had a chance to glance at it before he realized his mistake and came back for it. That day's entries, if memory serves, were:

**11.00a.m.** Breakfast. John Pigozzi
**12.30p.m.** Tennis
**2.00p.m.** Drinks at the Du Cap
**3.00p.m.** Free time with supermodel

The rest of the day was open.

When he returned for the date book we asked Eric whether Tim Bevan was going to be coming to the Festival; we hadn't seen him. Eric sighed. 'Alas, no,' he said, 'Tim can't take all this.'

**Joel Coen (right) and Ethan Coen (left) discuss a scene with Tim Robbins on the set of *The Hudsucker Proxy***

**'It's, you know – for kids!';
Norville Barnes (Tim Robbins)
shows off his hula hoop skills**

***Posse* – the untold story of the Wild West.**

*Left to right:* **Jimmy J 'Little J' Teeters (Stephen Baldwin), Obobo (Tom 'Tiny' Lister Jr), Jessie Lee (Mario Van Peebles), Father Time (Big Daddy Kane), Weezie (Charles Lane)**

With PolyGram as Working Title's new financial godfather, Tim and Eric were only limited by their imagination and Working Title's development skills in terms of what movies they wanted to make. So then, no surprise that the first film they produced for Gramercy was *Posse*, an African-American Western, a subject about which they had no absolutely no clue – or so we assumed. *Posse* came out the same year Clint Eastwood won the Best Picture Oscar® for his Western, *Unforgiven*, and a year after Mario Van Peebles won national acclaim for directing *New Jack City*. The timing couldn't have been better, and the success of the film was modest but profitable. So with Tim and Eric's instincts proving themselves, Gramercy was off and running as the new kid on the block that released innovative, risky movies with a substantial advertising budget and a flawlessly executed marketing plan that bordered on the insanely brilliant.
**– Russell Schwartz, President, Gramercy Pictures 1992–99**

**Jessie Lee (Mario Van Peebles, left) and Papa Joe (Melvin Van Peebles) in** *Posse*

*Panther*: **Members of the Black Panther Party of Self Defense silhouetted against the night sky, including Judge (Kadeem Hardison), Tyrone (Bokeem Woodbine), Bobby Seale (Courtney B Vance), Cy (Tyrin Turner) and Huey Newton (Marcus Chong)**

**Jack Grimaldi (Gary Oldman) finds himself in a tricky situation with ruthless Russian hitwoman Mona Demarkov (Lena Olin) in Peter Medak's *Romeo is Bleeding***

# DAVID LIVINGSTONE
President of Marketing, Universal Pictures International

**Eric:** He won't last
**Tim:** Not a chance.

I wasn't actually in the room when this conversation took place as it was shortly after my first ever meeting with them.

My recollection, however, was that it was possibly the longest meeting I have ever had with them. About seven minutes. The conversation was typically intense.

**Eric:** You want to know about our films?
**Tim:** *Romeo is Bleeding?*
**Eric:** It was called that… but it's now haemorrhaging. *Romeo* is now haemorrhaging.
**Tim:** *Romeo* is on life support.

In the ten years that have followed this meeting there have been some lows, but a lot of highs. So in the tradition of *High Fidelity* here is the top five:

1. *Four Weddings and a Funeral's* opening weekend's box office. 'British comedies don't travel… you are wasting your time.' Well, thankfully it was too late by the time we heard this. It went on to gross $250m plus.

2. *Bridget Jones's Diary.* The sixth biggest opening of all time in the UK. And the only one of the top ten without either a dinosaur or an alien.

3. *Fargo* party in Cannes. Hours before the launch party in Cannes the $2,000 ice sculpture that was the party's centrepiece collapsed. Faced with disaster someone suggested that we use the blizzard machine they had in the car to turn the villa into a winter wonderland. Honest.

4. *Billy Elliot.* An eleven-year-old boy forsakes boxing for ballet during the miners' strike. On that synopsis, an impossible sell. But as the very first film from WT² it went on to gross $100m worldwide. Working Title at its best.

5. Being in Japan on a promotional tour for *Notting Hill* and witnessing Hugh Grant accept, with sincerity and conviction, praise for his performance in *The Shawshank Redemption*.

# RUSSELL SCHWARTZ
## President, Gramercy Pictures 1992–99

In 1992 Gramercy Pictures became the US marketing and releasing arm of all the PolyGram-owned production companies: Propaganda, Interscope, and, of course, Working Title, which provided the bulk of the films. I had worked with Tim and Eric over the years at previous companies – with Tim on *The Tall Guy* and *Map of the Human Heart* while at Miramax and with Eric on *Straight to Hell* while at Island.

The PolyGram/Gramercy model held much promise in 1992 and, in the truest sense of the entrepreneurial start-up, the best times were at the beginning. Working out of the same building in LA we developed a unique and vibrant working relationship, as it was simple to move around offices and trade, share and kick around campaign ideas with no need to schedule meetings – simply stick your head in and talk.

But I did find myself in a curious position given we were suddenly all thrust under the same corporate umbrella. At my previous companies, I could say to either Tim or Eric, 'Look, we bought your film, it turned out OK, is proving very tough to market, and this is the campaign we are doing' (i.e. 'like it or not'). Being indie producers at the time, these guys were so busy trying to set up their next project that marketing their films in the US was only important for a short time, because what was *really* important was getting the next film set up before the current one came out in the States and, God forbid, didn't work. They always had to be two steps ahead of themselves.

So a relationship that initially had a strong separation as producer vs studio, suddenly changed dramatically when we were all thrown together at PolyGram. My new role was as 'friendly adversary', where I would query them on their production choices and they in turn would dissect my marketing decisions. Needless to say, the mutual respect we had for each other allowed this newly defined relationship to work brilliantly over the ensuing years.

**Taking time out from playing Lucy Trager, Gwyneth Paltrow celebrates her birthday on the set of *Moonlight and Valentino* whilst producer Alison Owen (right) looks on.**

# ADAM BROOKS
## Writer, *French Kiss*

Nine o'clock on a Monday morning in March the phone rings and it's Lawrence Kasdan's agent calling to congratulate me. What did I do? I ask, suspiciously. He tells me that Larry has read my script *French Kiss* and wants it to be his next movie. Would I have dinner that night with Larry and Meg Ryan to discuss?

Hm…

A relative neophyte at A-list dinners, I call Tim Bevan in London. Should I go, all by myself, unaccompanied by official Working Title-like people? What if I screwed up, said the wrong thing, ordered the wrong food, broke into a sweat?

His answer was short and to the point: 'Fucking right you'll go'.

Fucking right I went.

After years of occupancy in development hell, the process of writing *French Kiss* was like a Cinderella story. It was barely five months earlier that Liza Chasin asked me if I wanted to write a romantic comedy for Meg Ryan, set in Europe. From that first moment, for whatever reason, everything came easily. I had always wanted to set a movie in Paris, and I thought up the basic idea at that first meeting with Liza. The rest I worked over the next few weeks, and pitched it to Meg Ryan. She said yes. Then, miraculously, I convinced everyone that for me to write a really great screenplay I, and my entire family, needed go to Paris to live. Which we did. I wrote the first draft in five weeks, a record for me, unmatched since. And then just a month after finishing, the call came from Kasdan's agent.

The only bump in the fairytale was a set of notes I received from one of the executives outside of Working Title. They were extremely annoying – deadeningly banal, and at the same time just intelligent enough that they couldn't be dismissed out of hand. They hovered over me, like a dark rumbling storm cloud.

I went to dinner that first night with Larry and Meg, incredibly nervous. Famous and powerful people stopped by the table every thirty seconds. Damp palmed, I was introduced. We ordered drinks. And then Larry began to speak.

'Before we start, I just want to deal with these…'

He held up the dreaded notes.

And then tore them in half.

In the early nineties, Working Title Films' presence in Hollywood was small – by the time we made *Four Weddings and a Funeral*, *Posse* had been our most ambitious film to date. When we screened *Four Weddings and a Funeral* at the Sundance Film Festival in January 1994, we knew we might have a minor hit on our hands, the buzz was we could make $20m! Michael Kuhn gave Hugh Grant and Elizabeth Hurley Concorde tickets to fly home from the screening, and this was the first time we had really experienced this kind of 'Hollywood' treatment. We didn't realize the tide was going to change quite so dramatically. The phone started ringing, and having had to really hound people for scripts, suddenly we were being sent scripts that weren't dusty from sitting on shelves! For a while, we made some questionable choices, but we eventually parlayed our great success into *French Kiss*. One of our first acquisitions was *Moonlight and Valentino*, and truth be told, the reason why we made *French Kiss*, our first 'movie star' movie, was because we met Meg Ryan for the lead in that film. She said no, but we got on well with her. When we came up with the idea for *French Kiss*, we went straight back to her, and this time she said yes.
**– Liza Chasin, President of Production US, Working Title Films**

*Opposite:* **Meg Ryan shelters from the heat on location in the Luberon on the set of *French Kiss***

*Overleaf:* **Meg Ryan and Kevin Kline pose as Kate and Luc in a Parisian café for a special shoot for the promotion of *French Kiss***

## DEBORAH HARDING
Post Production Supervisor, *French Kiss*

It was a hot day in the Luberon. I had gone to France to visit the set of *French Kiss* ostensibly to try to understand and then explain why we were carrying 750,000ft of short-ends, or unused film stock (in other words, wasted money), after only two weeks of shooting. Admittedly a pretty tenuous reason for a location visit – but it was a heavenly one. A fabulous French farmhouse in front of which, and under an arbour of magnificent trees, a rustic table was being dressed with all manner of deliciousness. Actually, not dissimilar to what the caterers had just fed us. No wonder the Accountant was complaining of gaining weight, it seemed, at the same rate we were accumulating short-ends.

I looked around. Tim was talking to the stars: Meg Ryan (I still have the shirt and the boots) and Kevin Kline (the belt is still in use though the boots – affectionately known for years as 'Kev's Boots' – are now for building purposes only). I envied Meg 'that' hairstyle (is that why her stylist was rumoured to be paid more per week than the French prime minister?) and Tim for the easy manner in which he chatted and laughed with them. Ah well, better get back to the short-ends. I looked around again at the luxury Winnebagos and trailers. Having been brought up under the most excellent-but-frugal tutelage of Jane Frazer on hand-to-mouth budgets this all looked very lavish, almost decadent. I was rather shocked to find myself feeling, well, almost Protestant about it.

**La vie en rose: Meg Ryan and Kevin Kline share a moment's relaxation with Lawrence Kasdan (right) on location in France for *French Kiss***

The day got hotter, the sky got bluer, everyone crammed in more delicious pastries and mercifully for me they managed to reuse 250,000ft (or thereabouts) of short-ends. But that day seemed like an epiphany. To me it symbolized a watershed in the career of Working Title.

# ANGELA MORRISON
## Chief Operating Officer, Working Title Films

I first met Tim and Eric in April 1992. The film business was experiencing yet another downturn. I was running business affairs at Palace Pictures, Working Title's competitor. However, Palace was bankrupt and there was clearly no future there for me.

Soon after joining Working Title, I discovered that the company's main ambition was to make as many films as possible in any given year, usually all starting principal photography at the same time, but in different countries – in 1994 that meant *Panther* and *Moonlight and Valentino* in the US, *Loch Ness* in the UK and *French Kiss* in France.

There was an imperceptible shift over time, which only those who lived through it can truly appreciate. It is impossible to say when, but Working Title changed from independent to mini-major in the course of a decade.

A defining moment in that change was *French Kiss*. This was the first big-budget movie that we had made. We were shooting in France with an A-list director, two A-list stars, an American producer and some American crew. It was my first real exposure to the Hollywood system and we were coming at it with our 'grass roots' independent filmmaking approach. The directing and casting deals took months to negotiate (I remember trying to finalize Meg Ryan's deal from a phone box at the Carlton during the 1994 Cannes Film Festival). Tim and Eric obviously wanted the business affairs done properly. We were, however, sailing close to the wind in terms of our experience at this level of deal-making and it was important that no-one outside the company realized this. Advice was sought, strategies were formed, we took a deep breath and took the plunge. This was our first shot at it and we had to get it right. It was also important that we retained our own way of working, to make sure that the end result bore the hallmark of a Working Title film. Many lessons were learned on that film that subsequently shaped the future of the company and how we make films.

**Hanging on the telephone: Meg Ryan clowns around on set**

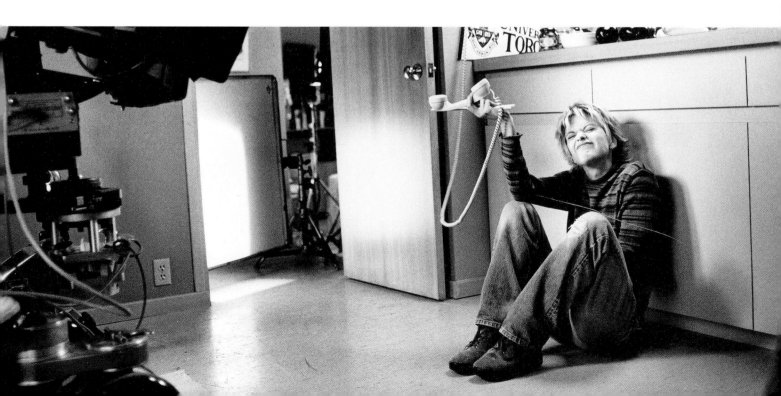

Great performances, a great soundtrack, a tireless public relations tour, and a subject matter that was not only timely but so emotionally strong that it had to be seen to be believed, all contributed to the success. Tim Robbins pushed all of our buttons in production and marketing, and as a director/producer, he was one of the toughest. But he gained our respect in spades. Tim and Eric supported this project through thick and thin – and it is that tenacity that creates great art.
**– Russell Schwartz, President, Gramercy Pictures 1992–99**

**Matthew Poncelet (Sean Penn) and Sister Helen Prejean CS (Susan Sarandon) in Tim Robbins's *Dead Man Walking***

# *Dead Man Walking*

### A Conversation

Elaine Goldsmith Thomas **(EGT)**, agent, Tim Robbins **(TR)**, director, Sam Cohn **(SC)**, lawyer, and Bart Walker **(BW)**, agent, on the making of *Dead Man Walking*.

**TR:** Susan [Sarandon] asked me if I would be interested in adapting the book. Over the summer [1994] I took notes, writing the draft in September. I sent it to Sister Helen who had many notes – it was like I had gotten my term paper back from my teacher. I had her in a habit and she said 'I haven't worn a habit since 1964'. I rewrote it, then we started sending it out.

**EGT:** I remember saying to you, 'So who do you want to play Matt?'. And you said, 'I sent it to Sean Penn yesterday'. About two hours later, you called me and said, 'Wanna hear something cool? Sean called and said, "Even though I have no interest in acting any more…"' He'd read the script and he said 'It broke my heart. I have to do it'. Did you know him?

**TR:** I'd met him a couple times.

**BW:** We had a first look deal with Working Title and when they got back to us it was an extremely enthusiastic response. Then the process of waiting for Bevan began.

**EGT:** All through November, Tim Bevan was telling us how good it was. Sam called Michael [Kuhn] who said, 'Yes, it's very good, I'm very excited about it'. But we still didn't have the green light.

**SC:** They seemed to be frightened about the commercial prospects.

**TR:** No one thought it could make any money.

**EGT:** This whole process was a great exercise in teamwork and faith.

**BW:** By December 21 Bevan said, 'If you need an answer today, it's no. It's too expensive'. He knew our number was eighteen. Then he took us to fourteen, then thirteen and a quarter.

**TR:** I called both Michael Kuhn and Alain Levy on [Christmas Eve] and I said give me a fucking answer. Please.

**BW:** Did you wish them a Merry Christmas?

**TR:** Of course.

**TR:** We trimmed and trimmed [the budget]… it was stripped bare below the line. Working Title were in the position of being able to not just reduce but basically eliminate our salaries out of the budget.

**EGT:** We're finding out where people are over the holidays so we can send them a script about the death penalty.

**Sister Helen Prejean CS, flanked by Susan Sarandon and Tim Robbins on the set of *Dead Man Walking***

I remember this scene well. We were in Slidell, Louisianna, and in the second week of shooting it was beginning to be hot. The scene had to do with my visit to one of the victim's families. Susan and Tim were great to work with – very collaborative all throughout the film.

**– Sister Helen Prejean CS, Author**

**BW:** Everyone in Hollywood is in Hawaii.

**TR:** To read on Christmas vacation! [Laughter] Who did we send it to?

**SC:** New Line, Paramount, Tristar, Universal, Warner Brothers, Capitol, Castle Rock, Ciby 2000, Columbia, Jake Eberts, Geffen, Gracie Films, Interscope, Miramax, Majestic, Savoy, New Regency, Twentieth Century-Fox, United Artists, Universal, Warner Brothers, Fox, New Line (again – second time), New Regency (we must've been desperate)… People loved it. But they were afraid.

**BW:** In the end, I mean this is a Working Title celebration… in the end Working Title said yes.

**SC:** The other perspective is they brilliantly got us to reduce an unbelievable percentage.

**TR:** Let's not also forget, they played on my relationship with the lead actress. They leveraged my relationship with the lead actress to bring down her fee, and my fee and Sean's fee.

**EGT:** And most importantly our commission. [Laughter] Everybody in town said how smart and great and brilliant it was and they were afraid of it. Not only commercially but also because of the politics at a time when most Americans supported the death penalty. So it wasn't an easy sell. In the end, it is noteworthy that we had to go outside of America to do a movie on an American issue.

**TR:** Any time I hear how Hollywood is so political and left-wing, I remember that.

**EGT:** Three people helped you here: Sam Cohn, Bart Walker and Tim Bevan.

**TR:** And you.

**EGT:** I was smart enough to get those guys involved!

**TR:** Look, Working Title just wanted to make money and there's no reason they shouldn't be like that. It's a business.

**EGT:** I will applaud Working Title forever. I don't necessarily applaud their methods or the helplessness of staring at the phone and not wanting to talk to you, it was really heartbreaking. But it was one of the most memorable times because the reward was so beautiful.

**BW:** What were they [Working Title] like during production?

**TR:** They totally left me alone, even through the editing up in the country at my house. I had everything stocked up there in our garage with my editor in the guesthouse. One of the greatest parts was this beautiful, elegant, creative development that happened on the album which was really humbling because some of my heroes were coming up with such beautiful songs – Springsteen, Johnny Cash… I remember someone saying, 'You wanna come out, there's someone on the phone for you' and I came out and the voice said, 'Hello, this is Johnny Cash' and I was like, 'Oh my God! It's one of my heroes!'.

**BW:** Michael [Kuhn] impressed me when he said, 'This is a very serious, complex, important piece of work and before saying how much I'm gonna spend on it or how I'm gonna market this film, I wanna be able to think before responding'. His methodology was to create a core concept and come up with a couple of fundamental sentences about the film from which all the marketing materials (trailer, poster, etc.) would emanate.

**TR:** A lot of more left-wing people came up to me and said there was too much of the murder in the end. But because of that Sister Helen tells me, it's become a great way for people to come to this issue. When she is giving talks, she'll show the film and she says it tills the soil for her to be able to talk to them about it. She feels that this movie is directly related to a sea-change. The opinion poll started to shift… it was eighty-five per cent for the death penalty before the movie came out, now it's sixty-five per cent… It has had a profound effect… That for me is the most humbling thing about [what] we were able [to do] with this movie…

I wanted to bring them to a place where they saw everyone as human beings. On the left, people tended to demonize the victims' parents making them into crazed people that want to see blood and vengeance. That's not true. They have a very human feeling of wanting to take a life for the life of their loved one. That, I can respect. And on the right, they want to make all the people who are against them into these irrational, hypersensitive people… and the truth is somewhere in the middle for both sides. And it pissed people off – I think that's the key – if you can piss people off and entertain them at the same time…

**EGT:** Then you're doing something right?

**TR:** You're doing something right.

**Tim Robbins directs Susan Sarandon on the set of *Dead Man Walking*. Roger Deakins, Cinematographer (centre) looks on**

# FRANCES McDORMAND
*Actress, Fargo*

**Frances McDormand and Joel Coen on the set of *Fargo***
The first time I was on the set in costume, I just sort of stood on the periphery, drinking a coffee until gradually people realized it was me. We, Joel and I, and everyone really had a blast with *Fargo*.
**– Frances McDormand, Actress**

William H Macy, not pictured, is trying out a local-dialect Sven and Ollie joke on Frances McDormand and Joel Coen. McDormand and Macy fought throughout the picture, especially after Macy learned that she'd tried to have him fired.
**– Ethan Coen, Filmmaker**

Having worked together with Eric Fellner on *Hidden Agenda* we all merged again on the filming of Joel and Ethan's *Fargo*, our most fruitful collaboration. It was truly a 'family picture' for us. Joel and Ethan had written many of the parts specifically for actors they'd worked with before and a lot of the crew were repeat collaborators. The entire process was a joy and the final product one of the best any of us had worked on.

Almost a year after its release, we were all invited to attend different awards festivities in its honour. We all rode to the Oscars® together drinking champagne, calling our mothers, and stopping at a nearby Burger King for a quick pee – gowns and all.

We've all travelled to many decadent places alongside Mr Fellner and Mr Bevan, tasting the good life and celebrating cinema and all the strange people that world attracts and harbours. Not unlike us all I guess.

**On the set of *Fargo***
Cinematographer Roger Deakins (front left) prepares to turn over on a patch of snow during the making of the motion picture *Fargo* while assistant camera Andy Harris (front right) concentrates on keeping his hands warm. Boom operator Peter Kurland stands by in case the snow should make noise. Director Joel Coen (back left) thinks about his postcode.
**– Ethan Coen, Filmmaker**

Oh look at them all! In their element. We went farther and farther north as the snow began to melt and we were down to a small crew by Grand Socks ND. It was good old days!
**– Frances McDormand, Actress**

**Marge Gunderson (Frances McDormand) approaches the overturned car in the snow**
I never get involved with the writing of scripts with Joel and Ethan. Though on *Fargo* I did offer one suggestion that they used – the 'I think I'm going to barf!' line. I also suggested they cut the Mike Yanagata scene. Okay. I was proved wrong on that one.
**– Frances McDormand, Actress**

*Above:* **Snowmaking on the set of *Fargo***
Whilst normally North Dakota can be guaranteed to have a huge snowfall, this particular year there was virtually none, so the SFX boys had to work their magic to turn Brainerd into the wintry landscape that epitomizes *Fargo*. Never depend on the weather!
**– Jane Frazer, Head of Production, Working Title Films 1990-2000**

*Below:* **Marge Gunderson (Frances McDormand) – *Fargo*'s finest policewoman**
Loved this outfit. Kept me very warm. All official North Dakota police wear which is weather appropriate. Plus the wig and pregnant pad and silicone fake breasts. I was never cold! Mary Zophres, our costume designer on *Fargo*, did have to make the maternity uniform however. They weren't doing anything so attractive at the time.
**– Frances McDormand, Actress**

*Opposite:* **Jerry Lundegaard (William H Macy) can only watch as his best-laid plans unravel before his very eyes**

# RICHARD CURTIS
Writer, *Bean*

### What was the background to the film of *Bean*?

What I find most interesting about the film is how true it is to its roots. In its beginning is its end. When Rowan Atkinson and I wrote the original *Mr Bean* sketches, they were three silent sketches for the stage, actually for three different characters – Rowan in church trying to eat sweets during the sermon and falling asleep, Rowan cheating and Rowan going to bed. They turned out to be by far the funniest things in Rowan's stage show, because his simple genius was on show and the audience felt they were watching something that no one else could do. No one else of our generation could do what Rowan did visually.

Years later, we had the idea of creating *Mr Bean* by joining these sketches together, pretending it was the same guy. This turned into a half hour-special for television and having done one, we started to do more.

I then became too busy, and handed over the writing of the TV shows to Robin Driscoll. I had been a huge fan of his in a show called *Cliffhanger*, and he really understood the Bean character. So when we decided to do the film, Robin and I wrote the script together. It turned out to be terrifically hard to get the concept of the film right, and we had a lot of meetings about what kind of film it should be. How much should we reveal? Should it be silent or not? I decided if we set it in England it would never really work, and finally we decided on this terribly simple *Uncle Buck*-type structure, of just taking him to the US and adding a third dimension – Bean interacting with a family for the first time.

Then it was a long script-writing process. There was one draft where Mr Bean said nothing, another where Mr Bean said huge amounts and I'm sure there was one where twice as much happened. Finally, after a couple of years, we felt we had a quite straightforward, good script. Then Mel Smith [who was directing], Rowan, Robin and I went back to the Chelsea Barracks, where *Mr Bean* had originally begun, to rehearse the sketches. We spent five days going through the set pieces of the film and rehearsing them as if for the stage.

And the odd thing is that, to my mind, the eighteen best minutes of *Bean* are those eighteen minutes we did in rehearsal. The actual jokes in the film are exactly the jokes we worked out then, with no props – destroying the picture, the wet trousers, the falling asleep. So in the end, the whole movie-making machine – script, casting, directing, editing – succeeded in communicating something very close to what *Bean* started as – a great silent comedian being simply funny.

Mel and Rowan managed to convey on screen what Rowan does best, and that is rarely achieved with comedians on film.

*Left to right:* **On the set of *Bean*: Mr Bean (Rowan Atkinson) can't wait to take on Hollywood with his bare hands; Director Mel Smith shows Rowan Atkinson how to make a gun with his hands; Mr Bean (Rowan Atkinson) tries the gun routine and attempts his best gangster impression; Mr Bean's turn at playing the Thanksgiving Turkey was not exactly director Mel Smith's idea of a joke**

Tim and Eric never said it would be easy marketing their films. At least with *Bean*, I thought a little of the pressure was off since the US was to be the last market to open and the film had already grossed $200 million worldwide. In other words, everyone assumed the film would fail in the States. Outside of a small following on Public Broadcast Television, Rowan Atkinson was all but unknown and certainly completely unknown to the eight to fifteen year-old boys that we determined were our target audience. To compound this, Rowan's comedy was really based on extended skits, not the stuff of one-liners that fit so well into a thirty-second television spot. We solved it by producing thirty-second cut-downs of the best scenes – what we called 'Bean moments' – and let the comedy play rather than going the conventional route of a quick comedy montage. Once audiences became familiar with the kind of physical comedy Bean excelled at, we were able to go the more normal 'close the sale' route. It worked, I breathed a sigh of relief, and Tim and Eric were able to point to their brilliant production.
**– Russell Schwartz, President, Gramercy Pictures 1992–99**

**Be Afraid. Be Very Afraid.
Mr Bean (Rowan Atkinson)
hits Tinseltown**

# RUSSELL SCHWARTZ
## President, Gramercy Pictures 1992–99

The Coen Brothers are to Working Title what bread is to the table – a staple. It is always something you want, it comes with many different tastes, and is rarely stale when you pay for it. The Coens are about innovation and longevity and Tim and Eric have made many films with the brothers, both successful and not. My theory? Given the amazing filmmakers that they are, if you stay with them long enough, the dividends will pay.

Their sense of humour, comedy, drama, violence, story and flair are unique in our movie world and to work with them was enormously fulfilling, yet everything about them defies the norms. Their films never 'test' well, the numbers always look depressing, there are a thousand things you want to suggest that should be changed, but in the end they are much more right than wrong, even when they gleefully admit they're not sure either.

*Opposite:* **Jeff Bridges as The Dude in *The Big Lebowski***

*Below:* **Roger Deakins filming Jesus Quintana (John Turturro), on the bowling set**
Working with the great Roger Deakins on a Coen Brothers film is as close to summer camp as you can get.
**– John Turturro, Actor**

*Opposite:* **Busby Berkeley meets the Coens. The Dude (Jeff Bridges) helps Maude Lebowski (Julianne Moore) perfect her bowling technique in the dream sequence**

*Left:* **Joel Coen (right) and Jeff Bridges on the Fantasy set**
Joel Coen choreographs 'The Dude'! Boy Movie! Hilarious and some of Mr. Bridges' (and others') finest work. But BOY MOVIE!
**– Frances McDormand, Actress**

*Right:* **Roger Deakins on the Fantasy set of** *The Big Lebowski*

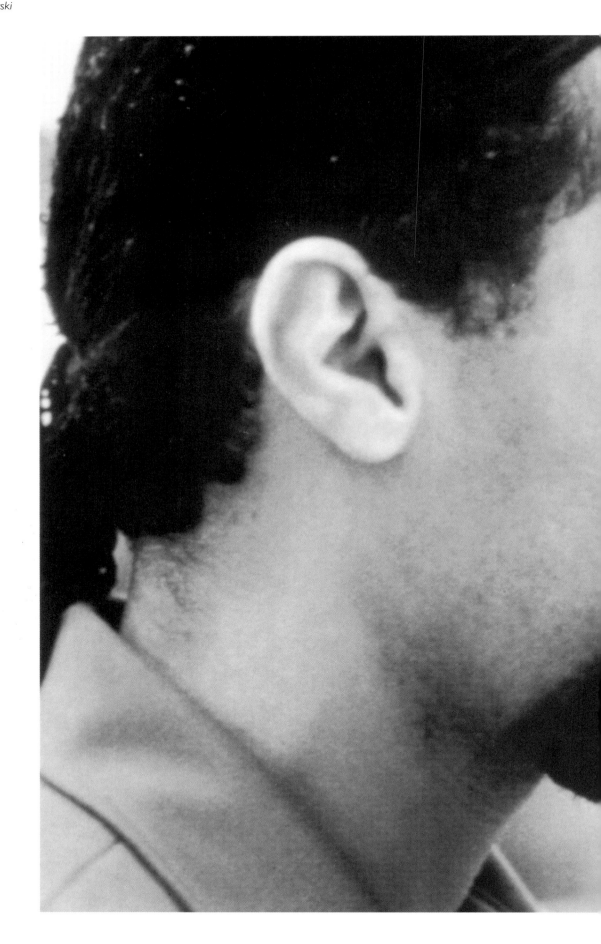

**Jesus Quintana gets ready
to bowl in *The Big Lebowski***
Bowling ball: what can I say –
this picture says it all. Jesus'
psychological gesture.
**– John Turturro, Actor**

## PETER HEWITT
### Director, *The Borrowers*

There are two Arrietty Clocks in *The Borrowers*. During the finale of the film, thousands of the little rogues scare the stuffing out of Ocious P. Potter, played by John Goodman. Three little four-year-olds – Molly Hewitt, Daisy Bevan and Indigo Lewin – came along to be Borrowers for the day. Borrowers have quirky, fun, borrowed names like Spiller, Peagreen, Minty, Swag. So the girls picked names. Daisy was 'Bead', Indigo was 'Sprout' but what about Molly? 'Arrietty,' she said. 'But we already have an Arrietty, sweetheart.' 'It's Arrietty or I'm going home with Mum.' Arrietty it was and if you look closely you can see them by Ocious P. Potter's giant left shoe.

**Gemma Jackson stands amongst the life-size retro props on the set of *The Borrowers***

After working on early Working Title films such as *Paperhouse* and *Chicago Joe*, several years later I was given the biggest design challenge of my career so far: Peter Hewitt's film *The Borrowers*. A designer's dream, an intriguing tale and a flight of fantasy. For many of us it was less a learning curve and more of a vertical hill!

**– Gemma Jackson,
Production Designer**

**Director Peter Hewitt (centre) explains a scene to Arrietty Clock (Flora Newbigin) amongst the life-size toy soldiers on the set of *The Borrowers***

**Pod Clock (Jim Broadbent) in the Lender family's kitchen in *The Borrowers***

The great thing about making *The Borrowers* was that it brought out the child in us all. The giant props and sets seemed to stimulate in us the awe and wonder of childhood. Seeing the world from a wholly new perspective encouraged us to play 'Let's pretend' on a grand scale, and our having such fun made it a bit more likely that the audience would enjoy themselves too. **– Jim Broadbent, Actor**

*Clockwise from top left:* **On the set of** *The Borrowers:* **John Goodman in make-up; Director Peter Hewitt shows John Goodman how to listen for Borrowers; Ocious P. Potter (John Goodman) in** action; **Officer Steady (Hugh Laurie, left) and Exterminator Jeff (Mark Williams) shelter under umbrellas between takes, with Ocious P. Potter (John Goodman) behind them**

*Left:* **Costume Designer Marie France's drawings for Arrietty**
*Right:* **Flora Newbigin as Arrietty Clock**

*Below left:* **Tom Felton as Peagreen Clock** *Right:* **Costume Designer Marie France's drawings for Peagreen**

I didn't really want to work on *The Borrowers* because I knew so little about Visual Effects – I kept suggesting more appropriate people to Jane Frazer, but they were determined that Michele Tandy and I should do it. Despite this, I'm very glad that I did because I learnt so much. The achievement by Gemma Jackson, Peter Chiang etc was phenomenal for the $29 million budget. It was a huge relief when the Producer, Rachel Talalay, eventually joined us – she literally arrived in the middle of a storyboard meeting, and after five minutes passed me a small slip of paper which said – 'We're screwed!' At last, someone could see how insanely ambitious we were trying to be. But with crisis meetings at least three times a week, we got there.

**– Mary Richards, Line Producer**

*Right:* **Storyboards for *The Borrowers* show the miniature Arrietty and Peagreen Clock using clothes pegs as an innovative form of transport**

# SHEKHAR KAPUR
## Director, *Elizabeth*

A man's journey through this life could probably most aptly be described as fate. And yet, at each crossroads, one's life seems to be prescribed by a moment of madness: illogicality.

There was no reason for me to have directed *Elizabeth*. I had never worked in England before, I'd never spent more than $1 million before, I'd never worked outside my home in India before. And, after all these years, I still have not discovered why Working Title offered me *Elizabeth*. Why they entrusted a film on the greatest icon of Britain to a relatively unknown director from India. I have asked, but never really got an answer. Only one answer: madness and fate.

Every company is a series of individuals. Two particular individuals in this company held my hand. Gave me confidence and then, quite unreasonably, allowed me to run wild: Debra Hayward and Tim Bevan.

And run wild I did. Breaking every rule in the grammar book of cinema, revelling in absolute freedom. And not once did either of them try and contain me. Yes, there was always advice. Yes, there was always constructive criticism, especially from Debra. But mostly what I remember was active encouragement, like parents encouraging a child to play. Ensuring, though, that he does not hurt himself.

Debra has since become a close friend. Tim? Well… Scratch the surface and you'll find Tim Bevan deeply loyal and affectionate towards all his directors. But the one way you are absolutely sure that Tim wants to work with you again is when he will never completely allow himself to be free with you. Because he knows that in a future film he may have to fight you very aggressively. Working Title spoiled me. I thought this was Hollywood. I was so wrong. This was home. Hollywood was a battlefield. I wish you had made me street smart before you let me out into the wild.

So, once again, fate. Once again at the crossroads. Once again into the madness.

*Opposite:* **Elizabeth I (Cate Blanchett), dancing the galliard**

*Left:* **Debra Hayward, Head of Film, Working Title Films UK and Director Shekhar Kapur on the set of *Elizabeth***

## MICHAEL HIRST
Writer, *Elizabeth*

I was working on a screenplay about Queen Victoria for an American studio, when Tim Bevan, who I've known for years, called me into the Working Title offices. 'For God's sake,' he said, 'can't you think of a more exciting monarch?' From this brief conversation, *Elizabeth* was born.

I had already written several drafts of the screenplay before Shekhar Kapur was brought on to direct – a brilliant decision, though a taxing one. Shekhar, as those who know him will attest, is a gruelling taskmaster and together we unpicked every stitch of the script and held up each scene to the light, the better to count its faults.

Eventually, miraculously perhaps, we had a draft good enough to cast from. At that point I informed Shekhar that I was going to France for a week's holiday with my family. Much to my surprise he arranged to come with us, in order to go on working. At which point my wife enquired whether I was married to her or to Mr Kapur.

Generally speaking, neither producers nor directors want the writer on set. Shekhar – and Working Title – were different. Actually, Shekhar told me that if I wasn't there to defend changes to my lines, he would happily permit the actors to do so. There was also some dirty work to be done!

Christopher Eccleston was playing the Duke of Norfolk. We wanted some way of showing his absolute power over people. We were also looking for a different sort of erotic scene, where the erotic element can often be created by the introduction of a third person. So we thought of a scene in which Norfolk's mistress is making love to a beautiful young man – when Norfolk walks in on them. But instead of being angry or offended he ignores them, signs some letters, then sits beside them on the bed while his mistress – still during congress – flatters and fawns upon him, being utterly within his power to dispose.

Shekhar told me to take the scene to Christopher, who hated it, and said there was no way he would allow himself to appear impotent. This was the very opposite of our intention but Christopher was not to be persuaded, and told me that if I even mentioned the idea again he would break my head open – or words to that effect. I was impressed with this warning, and the manner in which it was issued, but Shekhar, to his credit I suppose, was not, and sent me right back in to speak to Mr Eccleston about it once more. I think in the end we got away with a little bit of limb thrashing, but of the conventional sort.

In the end, despite my early misgivings, I loved being on the set. I think perhaps that initially I had a fear that, if I saw too many of the nuts and bolts of filmmaking then it would lose the element of magic which it has had for me since I first saw Cocteau's *La Belle et la Bête*. As Henry James said when discussing the workings of allegory, 'When the mechanism alone is visible, the ends to which it operates become a matter of indifference'. But a strange process actually occurs in filmmaking. The film that is being made is always being shadowed by another film, the film that it really is, or has the potential to be. And in the end, somehow, and if the film is any good, then all its nuts and bolts, its stitchings and threads, vanish into this other object as it emerges into the light.

Opposite: **'All of what I am. It is you' Elizabeth I (Cate Blanchett) and her lover Robert Dudley, Earl of Leicester (Joseph Fiennes)**

# ALEXANDRA BYRNE
Costume Designer, *Elizabeth*

'I will work you to exhaustion and beyond.' I felt challenged but inwardly confident of having stamina beyond average…

It was week one, pre-production on *Elizabeth* somewhere between Lacock House and Dover Castle (a rare event for a costume designer to be invited to join the bone-rattling minibus experience of a preliminary location scout). Shekhar was mid-flow on an inspirational discourse on Elizabethan conspiracies when he paused and calmly laid down the challenge. It was clear that working on *Elizabeth* was going to be a unique experience – a creative gift, a fantastic opportunity and an exponential learning curve.

A snapshot of this: a rather vague suggestion of a buying trip to India. Four days later I was sitting in the breakfast room of the Delhi Hilton. Jet-lagged, I watched guests negotiate their way through an extraordinary buffet, accommodating tastes ranging from chocolate muffins, kippers and muesli, to fragrant rice and marmalade. I prayed my shopping trophies would be equally eclectic and as startling as some of these combinations. In three days we bought buttons, braids, bullion brocades and boults of featherweight cottons in sufficient quantity to provide a core supply for what was to become an omnivorous workroom in Brixton.

An overnight return flight, and into a production meeting at Working Title (stamina still holding!) for heads of department to present progress reports. It was here that I really became aware of the 'workings' of Working Title – to give total support and artistic nurture, to create an environment where Shekhar could grow and develop his film. I was part of an organic process where the creative team was both protected and supported – free to focus and deliver Shekhar's vision.

If 'workings' is one area, then timing is another. Two-thirds of the way through shooting, the look of Elizabeth's court was established and I needed to change direction and re-focus towards the darker court of Queen Mary. A tired and travelled team, an exhausted workroom, a wobbly budget and a whole new court to conceive… Tim Bevan's curiosity took him to the Brixton workrooms while I was away on location in Northumberland. A brilliant piece of timing – luck/instinct/experience – his enormous enthusiasm and support was the catalyst to swing me away from taking the safer and less strenuous options, and on to pushing as far as we could go. Kathy Burke may lay any grievances for her corset at Tim's door!

*Elizabeth* was an extraordinary and wonderful journey – a benchmark in my career. I had reached 'exhaustion and beyond' and I had produced work of which I will always be proud – it had been a privilege for me to be part of Working Title's team.

*Opposite:* **Fit for a queen: Cate Blanchett has a final costume adjustment on the set**

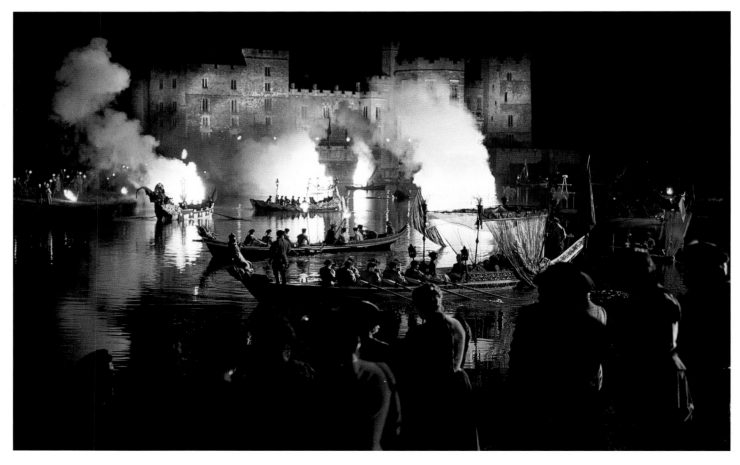

# REMI ADEFARASIN, B.S.C
Cinematographer, *Elizabeth*

I love cinema. For me, cinema is magical escapism, learning about other lives, going to places and situations that I would never encounter. Choosing which story I get involved with is always difficult. I need diversity and humanity.

The three films I have shot for Working Title are *Elizabeth*, *About a Boy* and *Johnny English*. These are hugely different films yet have one thing in common, they are popular. For me, shooting a film is a large undertaking. It is more than a job but a part of my life. It really hurts when a work goes by without being seen. Working Title has the skill to take diverse movies and make them successfully without selling out to commercialism. My first film with Working Title was *Elizabeth* directed by Shekhar Kapur. That alone says something about the company, getting an Indian director to make a serious film about an English monarch. On *Elizabeth*, the heads of departments got together well before the shoot started and talked about all the story and visual aspects of the film. We all wanted to make a powerful story but wanted all strands of the tale to weave tightly together. The sets, the costumes and make-up, the light and framing all had to be unified. The shoot was very hard work but very satisfying. We all felt we were collaborating in a very special way and making a very special film. The first part of the shoot was on location in the north-east of England. We often left the hotel at 6a.m. to travel for an hour to the location. We would then rehearse quietly and define the meaning of each scene. Getting to the essence was always the first thing on Shekhar's mind. The second was telling it visually and differently to what you might expect. The whole team enjoyed his approach and I loved his use of philosophy to distill the essence. Every day he would tell me to be brave. At 11p.m. after watching rushes, he would say, 'Remi, you were brave'. He was the same with us all I guess. The producers were brave too!

*Opposite:* **A Midsummer's Night Pageant: the Art Department's beautiful Night Regatta storyboard (above) is brought to life (below) in** *Elizabeth*

Working Title realized the potential of visual effects as a film tool outside the realm of science fiction or fantasy films. In 1998 on Shekhar Kapur's *Elizabeth*, a small visual effects team completed shots including a harrowing burning at the stake and subtle set extensions for sixteenth-century England. The film presented the opportunity for visual effects technology to blend seamlessly into a period drama.
**– Peter Chiang,
Visual Effects Supervisor**

*Below, left to right:* **Burning at the stake sequence in** *Elizabeth*: **setting up the shot; final touches; setting the martyrs alight**

# CATE BLANCHETT
Actress, *Elizabeth*

**What are your outstanding memories of the making of *Elizabeth*?**

*Elizabeth* was one of the first films I made, and the first film I had made outside of Australia. At the time I was unbelievably naive about the way a film was put together; my naivety enabled me to be quite fearless because I didn't have a sense of consequence. My first thought after reading the script was 'this will be a big ego trip for someone', but didn't for a second imagine I would be doing it. Then I met Shekhar and it was this relationship that subsequently propelled me into it. Suddenly I found myself in a studio doing a screen test, wearing a terrible wig – it was the first I'd ever done. And then Geoffrey [Rush] was cast – someone I could completely and utterly trust, and in some ways a mentor for me.

Once I'd been cast, I thought 'Oh dear, is this my ego trip?!'. I arrived to do the first hair and make up tests with the wonderful Jenny Shircore. I told her 'I've seen all these pictures of her [Elizabeth] and I need to bleach my eyelashes and eyebrows'. Jenny was horrified, and gently tried to dissuade me. I said 'No, let's give it a go'. I also decided I needed a much higher hairline. So I shaved it back, then in order to fit the wig, and for the hairline not to start too abruptly, they bleached a band of my hair. At weekends, I would walk around Covent Garden with a cap on my head, completely lost, looking like I had alopecia. Finally, three quarters of the way through filming, I had an 'I'm so ugly' meltdown.

My outstanding memory of filming is of storming up and down long, dark corridors at Shepperton. Making the film was an exciting and fluid process. It felt crazy at the time, and everything positive that came out of it seemed fated and full of chance. When people ask me about *Elizabeth* and what a success it was, they forget it was a risk and no one really knew whether it was going to work or not. *Elizabeth* paid off because it was so unusual and uniquely itself. For me, I've taken the 'lucky bastard' quality that Working Title has, and it has subsequently followed me through. I had nothing to lose, and I have taken that from the experience. After a success, you can forget the risks, and start to play safe. This isn't always the best way. Tim is a smart producer, because he doesn't always wait until something is perfect – and he takes the adrenalin with him into production, which keeps everyone on their toes.

*Opposite:* **Elizabeth I
(Cate Blanchett) in her
exquisite Coronation Dress**

# VANESSA PEREIRA
Casting Director, *Elizabeth*

A great script that was only made better by risky casting and an iconoclastic director – to encapsulate the Working Title model, you go against the grain, trust your instincts and see what happens. I remember being part of the executive process that screened all the audition reels, which Working Title presented to PolyGram. Some of these reels had bigger stars attached, some quite hot at the time, but all palled when Cate's came on. And I knew it was going to be Hugh Grant time all over again. Cate Blanchett anchored this historic thriller (a genre we created as a marketing acronym) with a sublime performance that knocked audiences out of their seats. Everyone at Gramercy loved it because it was so fresh and unique, with plenty to work with – a breakout star, a new take on history, a gorgeous-looking film, an emerging director, Golden Globe® and Academy Award® fodder, and equally so, a great story.
**– Russell Schwartz, President, Gramercy Pictures 1992–99**

The first time Simone Ireland and I met Tim Bevan we had such an appalling meeting that we stole the pens and notepaper from the boardroom, thinking that we would never see him again! Consequently, we were shocked that we were actually hired six months later to cast *Elizabeth*. Originally we were employed for ten weeks and I can honestly say the whole process took ten months. But in my short time as a casting director, I cannot remember a more creative and collaborative process.

When we suggested Cate Blanchett we were suitably sheepish. We had met her six months before and were incredibly struck by her. At the time, she was a little-known Australian actress. There was even a suggestion that Shekhar and I would fly to Sydney for the night to see her performing in *The Seagull*. Anyway, the rest is now history and she was, and is, magnificent, and we were very proud to have been part of her rise and rise.

Shekhar, not really knowing any actors, was very trusting. More times than I care to remember he allowed me to offer to actors unseen but on his meeting with them would freak and be madly gesticulating behind their backs that they were so wrong but, suffice to say, ended up loving them and even writing extra scenes for them. When we were casting the 'dance teacher' I cast Wayne Sleep; Shekhar had in mind a 'sergeant major' type – they got on famously. The casting of the footballer Eric Cantona was very risqué but his role needed more presence than dialogue and he worked perfectly.

When we got to casting Anjou, the French cross-dressing prince, we were under some pressure to cast a 'name'. We had so far collated a cast who were fairly unknown in the film world, except for the legendary Lord Attenborough. I think it was Memorial weekend when it was suggested I should check out the availability of a certain A-list US actor. It was an appalling idea. Tim was on a plane so I could not discuss it with him, but the gods were with us and the US offices were closed, so when Tim was back on Monday I pleaded with him not to pursue this. He barked, 'So what do you think?'. I explained the character was French and we should go after a French actor, nothing worse than a cod French accent and a guy in a dress! He asked me to submit some ideas. I remember calling him as he was driving to the set in Newcastle. I said Vincent Cassel. He said, 'I asked for a fucking list'. I said that was it. Vincent was offered and accepted the film and flew in to meet Shekhar. I then had a distressing phone call from Shekhar. He had perceived Anjou to be French, but small and ugly. He and Vincent became firm friends.

*Left to right:* **The groundbreaking poster campaign for *Elizabeth*: Heretic (Cate Blanchett); Lover (Joseph Fiennes); Assassin (Geoffrey Rush); Traitor (Christopher Eccleston)**

**Oscar®-winning Make-up Designer Jenny Shircore puts the finishing touches to Walsingham's (Geoffrey Rush) beard on the set of *Elizabeth***

**Cate Blanchett's elaborate hairstyle is adjusted for the Midsummer Night's Pageant scenes in *Elizabeth***

**Shekhar Kapur directs
Elizabeth I (Cate Blanchett)
and the Duke of Norfolk
(Christopher Eccleston) in the
Lady Chapel, Whitehall Palace**

*Opposite:* **Cowboys Pete Calder (Billy Crudup, left) and Big Boy Matson (Woody Harrelson) in** *The Hi-Lo Country*

*The Hi-Lo Country* is one of my favourite movies that I was in. I think Stephen Frears did a masterful job. I loved working with Billy Crudup… he is a powerful actor who takes his work seriously but we managed to have a lot of fun. One of my favourite moments was during my character's death scene. The entire scene was shot on location in New Mexico but for some reason the moment my character was to die we ran out of light and had to shoot it months later in London on a soundstage. I have had to die in movies before and I hate it, but as the camera was shooting over Billy's shoulder onto me and I'm doing my best to act my heart out, Billy, instead of crying and consoling, was smiling at me saying, 'Go to the light, follow the light!'. It wasn't easy getting through that without laughing – you could say I died laughing… Stephen Frears was very patient.

**– Woody Harrelson, Actor**

**Director Stephen Frears (right) gives some horse riding tips to Woody Harrelson**
This would have to be the most unlikely of photographs. Stephen, in New Mexico for the cowboy picture, *Hi-Lo Country*, spent much time protesting that he was from London and while he did have a house in Dorset, knew NOTHING about horse and cattle and what was he supposed to do? Being Head of Production at Working Title Films often meant getting bad news from film sets around the world and working out with everyone what to do for the best. So one of the happiest calls I had was from the wonderful producer of *Hi-Lo Country*, Rudd Simmons, saying that the first shot of the film was completed – the sun was out, the cowboys had driven the vast herd of cattle over the hill and all was excellent. Stephen could do livestock – we knew it all along.
**– Jane Frazer,
Head of Production, Working
Title Films 1990-2000**

**Stephen Frears (left) shows
Little Boy Matson (Cole Hauser)
how to shoot a gun**
Next time get a picture of me without Stephen's f**king hand in my face! Thanks.
**– Cole Hauser, Actor**

*Opposite:* **Director Stephen
Frears (seated) and Producer
Tim Bevan on the set of *The
Hi-Lo Country***

MACLEANE FILMS LTD.

"PLUN⟨...⟩T & MACLEANE"

CALL SHEET NO.27.

DATE: Monday 20ᵗʰ October 1997

DIRECTOR:                    JAKE ⟨...⟩
PRODUCERS:                   ERIC ⟨...⟩
                             TIM B⟨...⟩
                             RUPE⟨...⟩

UNIT MOBILES:
ANDI BROWN (2ᴺᴰ ASSISTANT) ⟨...⟩
JAROSLAV VACULIK (LOC. MA⟨...⟩
JANA (TRANSPORT) 0602 367671 ⟨...⟩ 12
ZDENEK (TRANSPORT) 0602 353 ⟨...⟩
LIDA ORNUNGOVA (PRODUCTION ⟨...⟩

UNIT CALL: 07.30

EXTRA'S W/RBE(Barrandov) CALL: 03.30

EXTRA'S M/UP(Barrandov) CALL: 03.45

PRINCIPAL W/RBE CALL: 06.30

PRINCIPAL M/UP CALL 06.45

'We were fabulous and it was a bloody good laugh!'

**Will Plunkett (Robert Carlyle, left) and Captain James Macleane (Jonny Lee Miller) – highwaymen extraordinaire in *Plunkett & Macleane***

*Opposite: **Plunkett & Macleane** call sheet in noose*

## CRAIG ARMSTRONG
Composer, *Plunkett & Macleane*

Working with Jake Scott (Director) and Eric Fellner was a fantastic experience for me. It was a very creative time and I think you can hear through the score how much we enjoyed working with the *Plunkett & Macleane* director and producer.

When I first wrote the music to the ball scene I was really worried about Jake's reaction but as soon as he heard it and I saw the reaction on his face I knew it was going to be a good experience writing the score and working with him.

When we discussed using the Tiger Lilies, we spent an entire day listening to all their albums, which left us in a very strange head state, as anyone who's listened to them would understand. I think my programmer Stephen Hilton decided, very unusually, to go to St Andrews beach that day as the sun, for once, was shining. We came back in the early evening and I can remember writing 'Rebecca', which to this day is one of my favourite pieces of film music.

The hanging scene was filmed in Tyburn, London. When the tapes came up to Glasgow for me to score to there was this drum beat in the background which completely shocked Jake as he had deliberately filmed the visuals only on the day at Tyburn, he hadn't recorded any sound at all. We kept the drum beat in the score for that scene but no one could explain where it came from.

I thought Jake's visual treatment of the film was so beautiful and he has a wonderful interpretation and understanding of music.

## JINA JAY
Casting Director, *Plunkett & Macleane*

Samantha Morton met Jake Scott and declared she was only really interested in playing one of the boys. We agreed! The very youthful and beautiful Johnny Rhys-Meyers read his lines standing and blazing on the Working Title conference room table. Lesley Sharpe met Jake with an enormous bunch of bananas spilling out of her handbag. Russell Crowe liked the script but we did not return the agent's calls! Jake was fantastic about wanting to dip into the new wave of comedians just emerging from the stand-up circuit and or telly. Ben Miller and Xander Armstrong refused to travel economy because it was simply not method and so paid to drink champagne in business class.

Jake and I were united in our mutual passion for *Trainspotting* which had just been released when we commenced casting and, to a large extent, the film inspired our lead casting decisions. And once Bobby Carlyle was secured we all agreed Jonny Lee Miller would be perfect for the role of Macleane.

*Opposite:* **'Stand and Fucking Deliver!'**
**Lady Rebecca Gibson (Liv Tyler)**
**in *Plunkett & Macleane***

**Behind the scenes on the set of** *Plunkett and Macleane*:

*Opposite page, clockwise from above left:*
**Making a phone call between takes; setting up the banquet scene; Make-up Designer Graham Johnston applies Liv Tyler's make-up; Producer Eric Fellner (right), Actress Liv Tyler and Director Jake Scott discuss the next scene; Jonny Lee Miller gets wired up for a stunt**

*This page, clockwise from above left:*
**Relaxing in the sun; catching up with e-mails; Robert Carlyle has a cigarette and a cup of tea; Winterburn (Alexander Armstrong) films his own version of events, Lord Rochester (Alan Cumming) sits opposite; Chance (Ken Stott) with gouged out eye and cigarette.**

**Behind the scenes in *Notting Hill***
This was the stretch of Portobello Road where we were pelted with eggs by a shopkeeper who seemed to feel we'd had a bad effect on his day's trade. Honestly! All we'd done was build a railway line outside his front door. Roger looks like he's returning something to the Portobello Hot Food Centre, Richard has clearly just been to Safeway, and I must have a duvet at the very least in my plastic bag.
**– Duncan Kenworthy, Producer**

# RICHARD CURTIS
Writer, *Notting Hill*

*Above:* **Emma Freud and Richard Curtis on the set of *Notting Hill***
Richard Curtis consults his script editor, muse, inspiration, and the person who writes all the best bits of his scripts actually (including this caption).
**– Emma Freud, Script Editor**

### Where did the idea for *Notting Hill* come from?
The idea for *Notting Hill* came to me on a dismal rainy day on the set of *Four Weddings and a Funeral* sitting in a room with Corin Redgrave awake and James Fleet asleep. *Four Weddings* and *The Tall Guy* were both based on 'dream scenarios', and I was trying to think if I had any other romantic fantasies in the back of my mind. At the time, I used to have dinner every week in Battersea with my friends Piers and Paula and Helen and I suddenly thought – what would happen if I turned up one night with, let's say, Madonna, in their kitchen, to eat the traditional dodgy green curry. I also had a friend who had once shared a flat with a boy who was having an affair with someone very famous, whom my friend would sometimes casually pass in the corridor.

### What happened when Working Title got involved?
The good thing was that when I told them about the idea, Tim and Eric didn't balk about really going for it. When I said, 'It's got to be someone like Julia Roberts,' they said, 'Well that's definitely who we'll go for'. I think they knew it would automatically be an expensive film and it didn't matter to them.

### How did it move from that first idea to finished script?
It was actually a very hard film to write, probably because it was fundamentally so simple and so little happened. Any time I tried to expand the canvas a little, and go outside W11 into areas I didn't know about – scenes with Anna Scott's agent, or what it's like living in Hollywood – my writing became false.

*Below:* **Writer Richard Curtis (left), Director Roger Michell (centre) and Spike (Rhys Ifans) amongst the rooftops of *Notting Hill***

**Did you think there was a burden of expectation after *Four Weddings*?**
No. It's always so difficult writing any movie that the idea of the movie actually even getting made seems ridiculous – so worrying about whether or not it will eventually do well would be totally ridiculous.

**How did it get from script to screen?**
Once I had eventually finished writing, Duncan Kenworthy read it and we asked Roger Michell to direct it. On *The Buddha of Surburbia*, Roger had done this remarkable trick of bringing two extraordinarily different worlds together in a convincing way and this movie was also about a culture clash of sorts. Roger's also exactly the kind of director I like, finding truth in a situation is always his primary interest.

**Tell us a bit about the casting...**
We actually talked a lot about the casting of Hugh as our 'not famous' bookseller, because he had become a huge star in real life – but finally we saw sense and cast him anyway. Julia was the first and only person we asked to play the girl. The difficulty wasn't choosing her – it was whether she'd choose us. Roger, Duncan and I flew to New York to meet her. We shared one room at the Four Seasons Hotel, and all got changed into our suits like people nervously applying for a job. It was the first time we'd ever seen Roger in a suit – actually I think it was the first time I'd ever seen him in socks. Julia sort of interviewed us, and it seemed to go okay – but as we left her, I remember the last thing she said to Roger was, 'Good luck with your film'. In a state of silent terror en route to the airport, it seemed obvious to me that she meant 'I'm not going to do your film – good luck with it'. Eventually, before we got on the plane, I broke my silence and said to Roger, 'You know she's not going to do it'. He said, 'What do you mean?' 'Well the last thing she said was "Good luck with your film"', and he said, 'Yes – I'm doing *Titanic Town* before we shoot *Notting Hill*'. I'd aged a year in an hour.

**It's not easy being a famous girl: Anna Scott (Julia Roberts) rings for rescue whilst Spike (Rhys Ifans, left) and William (Hugh Grant) hover in the background**

## ROGER MICHELL
Director, *Notting Hill*

I'm on the intersection of Portobello Road and Kensington Park Gardens, it's a very busy market day, thousands of people are milling around buying artichokes and shouting at each other and slapping their children. Along with me there is a crew of around forty people (slimline, you see, I wanted us to keep a low profile). I've got two cameras, one on around thirty foot of track, and one right at the end of the track on a tighter lens. Every now and then people with big bags of avocados trip over the track and it needs re-laying, and the avocado people need reassuring. Somewhere in a house nearby I have the biggest female film star in the world waiting to come out into these crowds and strut her stuff. I can see the first assistant director, a handsome, ruddy-faced guy, standing staring at the hordes. He is pale as milk. I notice him dragging heavily on one of my Marlboro Lights, which is curious and disturbing behaviour in a non-smoker. I've got the writer squinting into a monitor, whingeing on about the precise colour of the orange juice that Hugh is about to throw over Julia's breasts. I've got the producer whingeing on about whatever the writer's whingeing on about. It's the middle of May, and without warning the sun is obscured by a malevolent cloud straight from the bowels of hell, which begins to shoot walnut-sized hailstones directly at our heads. And at this moment, at this precise moment, I think, where the fuck is Eric Fellner?

**The old orange juice trick: William Thacker (Hugh Grant) bumps into the girl of his dreams, Anna Scott (Julia Roberts), on the Portobello Road**

**Christmas in May on the
Portobello Road: snowmaking
in *Notting Hill***

**Behind the Scenes on *Notting Hill***
Julia is just in a shirt, and then in a
bath, while Hugh is in a bathrobe –
probably just before revealing his pecs
in the bedroom scene. Richard seems
to be pressing his knees together in
sympathy as we listen to Hugh's story.
The scene of Hugh and 'the friends'
walking back down Portobello Road
after the restaurant opening was
eventually cut from the film. Stuart
Craig, our brilliant set designer, and
the World's Nicest Man, is revealing
the secret of his amazing, 3-D, 'forced
perspective' backdrop seen outside
the window of Tony's restaurant.
**– Duncan Kenworthy, Producer**

*Middle picture, left to right:* **Bella
(Gina McKee), Honey (Emma
Chambers), Will Thacker (Hugh
Grant), Bernie (Hugh Bonneville)
and Max (Tim McInnerny) walk
down the Portobello Road**
A memorable day for two reasons.
One, for the Portobello shopkeeper
who kept lobbing eggs at us, take
after take, until encouraged not to
by the huge security guard with gold
teeth. The other reason? Because the
scene never made it to the final cut.
I blame the egg man.
**– Hugh Bonneville, Actor**

Hugh Bonneville and I look so serious
because we saw this as a sort of up-
market *Reservoir Dogs* – possibly *Boat
Race Beagles*. Also, we were never
quite sure where the next egg from
a disgruntled shop-keeper was coming
from. Notice Hugh Grant making an
early move without realising how fast
Gina McKee can run in real life.
**– Tim McInnerny, Actor**

*Left to right across the pages:*
**Julia Roberts relaxes between
takes; Spike (Rhys Ifans) flashes
his winning smile; behind the
scenes outside Tony's
restaurant; Director Roger
Michell (far right) rehearses a
scene with Hugh Grant (in bed)
and Julia Roberts**

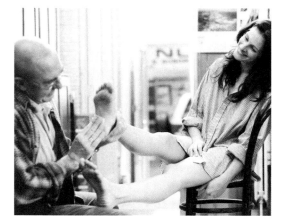

**Production Designer Stuart Craig on his 3D set with explanatory illustrations**

Top marks to the Art Department: in the deep background is a red London bus passing the end of the street. It was painted on a five-inch strip of cardboard mounted on a stick, and someone actually wiggled it along during the take. Who needs Industrial Light and Magic when you've got sticky-backed plastic and a bit of imagination? Not to mention a bored stagehand.
**– Hugh Bonneville, Actor**

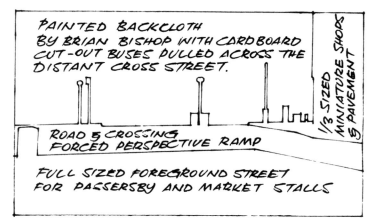

PAINTED BACKCLOTH BY BRIAN BISHOP WITH CARDBOARD CUT-OUT BUSES PULLED ACROSS THE DISTANT CROSS STREET.

⅓ SIZED MINIATURE SHOPS & PAVEMENT

ROAD & CROSSING FORCED PERSPECTIVE RAMP

FULL SIZED FOREGROUND STREET FOR PASSERSBY AND MARKET STALLS

'B' STAGE SHEPPERTON
The backing for INTERIOR TONY'S RESTAURANT (replicating the exterior location at Portobello Road and Golborne Road) Not a "translite" or blue screen but a little showing off of old fashioned skills.

**The *Notting Hill* cast and crew**
Clive Coote, bottom left, triggers the
shutter remotely while Mick Coulter,
just behind him, smiles at how easy it
is when you don't have to put lights
up. I prefer to think that Julia's leaning
towards her director rather than away
from me – but Hugh and Richard are
definitely up to no good. Our
wonderful and sadly missed camera
operator, Mike Roberts, is in the white
shirt over my right shoulder, and you
can pick out 'the friends' behind Roger.
Let's just ignore the attention-seeking
first AD in the background.
**– Duncan Kenworthy, Producer**

A casting director's job is all about
actors, watching them, meeting them,
talking about them, thinking about
them. When I start work on a film I
spend all my time with the director,
talking about the film and everything
else in the world and so much is,
sometimes unwittingly, revealed in this
relationship, to try to understand this
director person, their concept of the
film will often lead you to understand
their taste in actors, politics, humour,
their attitude to life, to people, so many
things. This odd compressed process
sometimes results in a real friendship
and that was so in *Notting Hill*, it took a
very long time to cast that long list of
characters. My abiding memory of the
film is Roger Michell, a wonderful
director of actors, an endlessly
interesting man and now my friend.
**– Mary Selway, Casting Director**

# 2000 onwards

THE PRESENT

BILLY ELLIOT
O BROTHER, WHERE ART THOU?
THE MAN WHO CRIED
HIGH FIDELITY
BRIDGET JONES'S DIARY
CAPTAIN CORELLI'S MANDOLIN
THE MAN WHO WASN'T THERE
ALI G INDAHOUSE
ABOUT A BOY
40 DAYS AND 40 NIGHTS
THE GURU
JOHNNY ENGLISH
NED KELLY
LOVE ACTUALLY
THUNDERBIRDS

# STEPHEN DALDRY
Director, *Billy Elliot*

I've noticed that people have worked up some great stories about how they fell in love with making movies. The childhood escapism, the *Cinema Paradiso* romanticism, or the psychological trauma that became the mother of their imagination is repeated with misty-eyed sentimentality throughout interviews with directors.

I have always felt the odd man out when asked, "What made me want to become a film director?".

As a child I never had any real interest in movies. I was a reluctant visitor to my local Odeon in Taunton, where the highlight of my adolescent celluloid experience was joining a competition ran by the local Gazette newspaper for a year's free tickets. All you had to do to win was sit through a screening of *The Return of the Pink Panther* and not laugh. As it turned out the competition was far too easy for all 150 contestants – who all ended up with free passes. I don't even remember using the pass after the desultory experience of *The Pink Panther*.

As a fifteen year old, glamour, excitement and sheer unadulterated adrenelin rushes were always to be found with the local youth theatre. Cinema was for anoraks with no friends.

So it took me by surprise that some years later when I was Artistic Director of the Royal Court Theatre, two anoraks named Tim Bevan and Eric Fellner took me out to lunch and asked me to forget all about this theatre nonsense and come and join them at Working Title.

It took me even more by surprise that I accepted.

But watching Tim and Eric both laughing and crying during the 'Billy Elliot Musical' workshop presentation the other day, I was struck by the thought that possibly these two were not obsessive film addicts after all, but in fact closet theatre junkies.

Maybe that's what I misunderstood during that fateful lunch. It was not an invitation to make films, but an offer for them to join the theatre!

**Stephen Daldry (centre) directs Michael Caffrey (Stuart Wells, left) and Billy Elliot (Jamie Bell) in the boxing ring, whilst choreographer Peter Darling looks on**

*Opposite:* **Jamie Bell on the set of** ***Billy Elliot*** **(which was originally titled** ***Dancer*****)**

## JON FINN
Producer, *Billy Elliot*

Due to pressure on the shooting schedule, we had been forced to drop this scene from the script. It was the dance between Mrs Wilkinson and Billy to 'I Love To Boogie'. However, my fellow producer, Greg Brenman, and I, along with everyone in the cast and crew, really wanted it in the film. So we all agreed to work an extra day (for no extra cash) as long as we finished by two o'clock in the afternoon so that everyone could watch a big England football match.

I'm holding a radio in the picture because our first assistant director wasn't available so I stepped in, which was great fun for me but probably less so for everyone else, especially Stephen Daldry.

We started at eight o'clock in the morning with Brian Tufano (Cinematographer) lighting the hall while Peter Darling the choreographer ran through the dance. Jamie Bell was very excited while Julie Walters was very nervous. By ten o'clock we were ready to start filming. This would give us four hours to shoot a really complex scene.

Just before calling 'turnover' on the first shot of the day the storm that was raging outside blew over one of our massive lights, which was providing daylight on an otherwise dark day. The light was smashed and it looked like the day was over before it had begun. There was a massive sense of frustration and disappointment.

We didn't have many options but Brian suggested changing to film in the other direction, which would be our only chance of getting anything at all. Unfortunately because of the position of the boxing ring Peter Darling had to butcher his choreography and vastly simplify his original idea. I think we all agreed we had nothing to lose. As the electricians began the re-light, Peter began re-working the dance and time continued to tick away. We knew that we wouldn't have time to do the tracking shots as planned and decided that Brian would have to go hand-held with the camera. In the end we decided to grab what we could at breakneck speed. We had originally scheduled a full twelve-hour day for this sequence but ended up having only two hours of shooting.

Every time I watch the film I think about the mayhem of trying to 'capture' that scene and am always frustrated that it seems so short but amazed that we got anything at all.

**Jon Finn gives Jamie Bell a piggy-back on the set of *Billy Elliot***
This picture was taken on the last day of shooting on *Billy Elliot*, it was a Saturday. In the foreground, myself and Jamie Bell while Stephen Daldry (Director) and Julie Walters have a conversation in the background.
**– Jon Finn, Producer**

## JINA JAY
Casting Director, *Billy Elliot*

The journeys to Newcastle always began fairly dramatically with myself throwing up outside King Cross station before boarding the train with Stephen Daldry, (Director), Jon Finn, (Producer) Greg Brenman, (Producer), Peter Darling (Choreographer) and his assistant Lynn for huge coffee fuelled gossiping sessions in the smoking carriage. The return journeys were usually more sober affairs because we were so bloody exhausted from seeing hundreds of very brave but stunned boys who had all been put through their dancing paces to music from 'The Entertainer' by Peter Darling when they would normally be playing footie.

The search for Billy happened in a relatively short space of time and with the enormous support and achievements of Shaheen Baig, Chloe Emmerson, Pippa Hall and Patsy Pollock, without whom the brilliant Jamie Bell would not have been found.

We met some amazing young boys. Jamie Bell appeared fairly early on in the search alongside another great boy, Lee Darville. Jamie had never worked on film but had been involved with the National Youth Music Theatre and was a regional tap-dancing champion. Stephen fell in love with Jamie whose mum, Eileen, was a gem. Stephen's instincts were absolutely right and the rest is history.

Julie Walters was only able to meet Stephen at her hairdressing salon so Stephen chatted to her during her cut and blow dry!

**Siren's Kiss: Ulysses Everett McGill (George Clooney) is seduced by the beautiful Siren (Musetta Vander) in *O Brother, Where Art Thou?***
To be part of such a wonderful movie was a dream come true. This particular set up captured the waif-like mystical seduction of the scene so well, that it made the whole experience seem effortless, dreamlike and easy to get lost in. At one point I realized, 'Hey, wait a minute, I'm the one who's supposed to be doing the seducing here!'
**– Musetta Vander, Actress**

**George Clooney celebrates his birthday on the set of *O Brother, Where Art Thou?* with the help of Ethan Coen (far left), Production Designer Dennis Gassner (second left) and Joel Coen**

The Soggy Bottom Boys (from left: John Turturro, Tim Blake Nelson, Chris Thomas King and George Clooney) bring the house down in *O Brother, Where Art Thou?*

George Clooney (left) and Tim Blake Nelson share a joke on the back of the tracking truck on the set

*Opposite above:* **Behind the scenes on the Chain Gang: convicts Pete (John Turturro, far left), Delmar O'Donnell (Tim Blake Nelson) and Ulysses Everett McGill (George Clooney) rehearse under the watchful eyes of Joel and Ethan Coen (far right) on the set of *O Brother, Where Art Thou?***

*Opposite below:* **Joel Coen (left) and Ethan Coen take a break from filming**

**Showgirl Lola (Cate Blanchett) wows her audience in *The Man Who Cried***

**Cate Blanchett with clapperboard on the set of *The Man Who Cried***

# LINDY HEMMING
## Costume Designer, *The Man Who Cried*

*The Man Who Cried* was a really interesting design project full of late-1930s period costumes, and set in Russia and France, with Johnny Depp, who I already knew, Cate Blanchett, Christina Ricci and John Turturro, and I had always wanted to work with Sally Potter. She has a real interest in design, and in the look of heightened reality which I love, and which one doesn't often get the opportunity to do. Also, she allows quite daring choices of colour and dramatic cinematography, which are the aid and benefactor of the costume designer. It was a very hard and exhausting project, and sadly did not do so well, but it's a film that I like watching to see all the things that we all, as a department, managed to achieve, and I really enjoy all the different costume occasions which the script demanded.

*Above:* **Lola (Cate Blanchett) and Dante Dominio (John Turturro) make a connection in *The Man Who Cried.*** Cate Blanchett's headdress is a nightmare version of my own hair in the morning…
**– John Turturro, Actor**

*Right:* **Suzie (Christina Ricci) in her showgirl costume in *The Man Who Cried***

**Sally Potter directs John Turturro in the opera scene**

Being an opera singer has always been a fantasy of mine. To get to do it in the company of Sally Potter, Cate Blanchett, Johnny Depp, Christina Ricci, on the stage of the Paris Opera, was a dream come true. Unfortunately I didn't get to keep the gold skirt.

**– John Turturro, Actor**

*The Man Who Cried* is a lament about loss, threaded through with song. The story, and its music, tells of the parallels between the fate of the gypsies and the Jews during the Second World War, and of the bitter choices faced by all exiles in the struggle for survival. Filming the opera scenes was one of the lighter moments of the shoot; vividly theatrical, technically demanding, and sometimes very funny. It was the last film lit by Sacha Vierny (maestro cinematographer of *Last Year in Marienbad* amongst many others). His feeling for light and shadow infused every frame. In this still, Cate Blanchett and Christina Ricci are partially hidden on the other side of the curtain as members of the chorus; Johnny Depp is out of sight somewhere on the stage with his horse, whilst John Turturro is the visible – and very audible – tenor. (Salvatore Licitra, who provided his voice, has subsequently become known as 'the fourth tenor', following his brilliant New York debut in 'Tosca'.) When I first approached Tim Bevan with the idea I'm not sure he realized what he was letting himself in for (it turned out to be a highly charged and challenging experience for everyone involved – but then what film is not?) but he responded to the impulse of the film with admirable alacrity. And I'm not sure how opera buffs have responded to the finished film, but Jewish exiles and Romany people do seem to feel it speaks (and sings) for them.

**– Sally Potter, Director**

**Rob Gordon (John Cusack) contemplates another top five all-time greats in *High Fidelity***

*The Hi-Lo Country* was in competition in Berlin. I flew home and then went back to Berlin because the film had won a prize. The Danish film *Mifune* had won a prize (I think collectively, for the acting). Afterwards the jury – in a rather mannish way – were egging me on to speak to the pretty actress who had received the prize on behalf of all the Danish actors. She had made a speech in what I came to realize was an American accent. At the time I was unable to find an actress to play the lead in *High Fidelity*. It's a story about a man who realizes he had lost through carelessness the love of his life so I was looking for someone special, someone who was younger than John Cusack but could stand up to him, could give as good as she got, bright like many young women I know. I found myself asking Iben Hjejle if she would like to be in a Hollywood movie. She looked at me as if I had suggested white slavery. I came back and tried to sound convincing as I explained, first to Tim, then to John Cusack, and finally to the Disney Studio, that I had met a Danish girl in Berlin and thought we should consider her for our film. She spoke American because as a child she'd spent a year in the US. Of course, she got the job and was terrific. To this day I've never met anyone who could pronounce her surname.

**– Stephen Frears, Director**

**Rob Gordon's (John Cusack) search for true love: kissing Laura (Iben Hjejle, below left) and Charlie Nicholson (Catherine Zeta-Jones, below right) in *High Fidelity***

*Left to right:* **Screenwriters Steve Pink and D.V. DeVincentis, author Nick Hornby and *High Fidelity* star John Cusack on the Championship Vinyl set**

D.V. DeVincentis – the guy in the hat – was one of the writers who adapted *High Fidelity* for the screen. I once asked him why the John Cusack character was called Rob Gordon in the film when, in the book, he was called Rob Fleming. I wondered whether Gordon was a more American-sounding name (the film was set in Chicago, whereas the book was set in Holloway). Or whether Gordon was a homage to the rockabilly singer Robert Gordon, or the venerable rock critic of the same name. D.V.'s answer was that he was in a hurry, and couldn't be arsed to look through a whole book for a surname. I learned a lot about the film industry in that moment.
**– Nick Hornby, Author**

I was super-tired when this picture was taken, otherwise I would have joined in this moment of apparent on-set fellowship.
**– Steve Pink, Sreenwriter**

I think this may be a photograph of a joke dying.
**– D.V. DeVincentis, Screenwriter**

When you sit on your own staring at a screen, it's very hard to get used to the sheer numbers of people involved in the film industry. I quite frequently feel embarrassed at the trouble and expense I seem to have put people to; everything on a set feels much less whimsical and much more professional than it did when I was writing the book.
**– Nick Hornby, Author**

**Rob Gordon (John Cusack) and Laura (Iben Hjejle) shopping for vinyl in *High Fidelity***

# MICHELLE GUISH
## Casting Director, *Bridget Jones's Diary*

With *Bridget Jones's Diary* we have the enviable task of casting one of the most popular literary heroines of the nineties. Aagh! Everyone, including newspaper journalists, had something to say about the process. When the decision was made to offer the role to Renée Zellweger it felt absolutely right even though she was not British. Renée has what I can only describe as an adorable quality which, for a character with as many phobias as Bridget, seemed to be a perfect balance. Then there we were again, casting that 'disparate group of characters' which this time were based on real-life characters. Aagh! No pressure then! At the read-through of the film we were filled with admiration when Renée, who had spent at least two months acclimatising herself into London and its literary world, read her entire role in a near-perfect British accent. When you consider that actors are not required to speak more than the dialogue in a single scene at any one time, it was a remarkable achievement. I also think we were incredibly lucky to have Colin Firth play Mark Darcy. The case rests.

*Above:* **'Genuinely Tiny Knickers'** and **'Scary Stomach Holding-in Pants very popular with grannies the world over...'**

*Left:* **'Hello Mummy!'** **Daniel Cleaver (Hugh Grant) falls for Bridget Jones's (Renée Zellweger) many charms in** ***Bridget Jones's Diary***

*Opposite:* **'Nice boys don't kiss like that!' 'Oh yes they fucking do'**

# DEBRA HAYWARD
Head of Film, Working Title Films UK

*Bridget Jones's Diary*: **From Development Hell to Cinema Heaven**

A meeting with author, Helen Fielding, resulted in our dissuading her from developing her cult diary as a sit-com for the BBC, and making it as a feature film. With that decision made, we were then confronted with the problem of how to bring her utterly original voice and the escapades of her eponymous heroine to the screen. (**Double Expressos drunk: 5,000.**) We were lucky enough to work with Helen Fielding, Andrew Davies and Richard Curtis on the screenplay, under the guidance of hilarious director, Sharon Maguire – the original inspiration for the character of Shazza. (**Pret-A-Manger Tuna Wraps consumed: 2,500.**) As the script neared completion, panic set in about the casting of Bridget – who would ever be able to play this character beloved by women the world over? (**Marlboro Lights smoked: 10,000.**) A petite blonde American with the strongest Texan accent imaginable was mad enough to take on the challenge. (**Pounds gained by Renée Zellweger for role: 20. Pounds gained in sympathy by Jonathan Cavendish: 20.**) As in so many films, the script continued to evolve during shooting. Hugh Grant's fantastic improvisational skills led to the creation of the movie's most infamous scene, namely the 'Big Pants' seduction in Daniel Cleaver's apartment (**Swooning Singletons and Smug Marrieds around the world: 100,000,000.**) After much laughter and some tears and many, many hours of work by the best possible cast and crew, *Bridget Jones's Diary* emerged and has gone on to become one of Working Title's most admired and successful films.

Flashforward three years and we are once more into the breach with the sequel *Edge of Reason*, where we will find out what has become of Bridget Jones after the end of the happy ending. (**Days of therapy required by all involved in order to undertake this crazy enterprise: 200 and counting…**)

**Liza Chasin, Head of Working Title Films LA (left) and Debra Hayward, Head of Film, Working Title Films UK** on the set of *Bridget Jones's Diary*

*Opposite:* **Renée Zellweger waits for the rain to stop between takes**

**Director Sharon Maguire (left) discusses a scene with Renée Zellweger and Hugh Grant in Bridget's flat**

It had been a particularly long haul – months (actually years) of script development, months (and then more weeks) of shooting and what seemed like several decades of editing. We were all nervous, any reactions of amusement at the film long since anaesthetised within the clinical confines of the cutting room. Now we were sitting gloomily in a New York cinema. A test audience was about to watch the film and give us a verdict. Thumbs up or thumbs down? We were in a roped off area, surrounded by glowingly healthy Universal executives. I sat between the film's director Sharon Maguire and Working Title's development supremo Debra Hayward. We were in this mess together. Sitting behind me, glowering dangerously, was the pulsating bulk of Harvey Weinstein. The lights dimmed, logos flashed onto the screen. The film started, but I saw nothing as I had my head in my hands. I heard painfully English references – doylies, turkey curry – and felt the audience's bemusement. My mind flicked over a barren landscape of alternative careers. And then it happened. A laugh. And then a roar. And applause. I looked up – Mark Darcy's reindeer jersey was the cause. Debra Hayward squeezed my arm with extraordinary power. Harvey laughed gigantically, flicked up his feet and kicked me solidly on the back of the head. I was in great pain, but we had a hit.
**– Jonathan Cavendish, Producer**

**Actress Renée Zellweger (left) and Director Sharon Maguire on the set of *Bridget Jones's Diary***
What I remember about this is that it was around 3am, on a night shoot and was taken just after a bout of girlie wrestling on the stunt mattresses on which we're perched.
**– Sharon Maguire, Director**

**Renée Zellweger surrounded by camera equipment on the set**

When I met Tim Bevan for the first time, I was a brand-new agent taking my first business trip to London. I was so junior that I had to pay for my own ticket. Before he agreed to meet me I had to fax him my then quite unimpressive client list. I think the meeting only happened because I raved about *The Tall Guy*. Tim launched into a speech about what he needed from American agents. As I recall it was all about convincing well-known actors to work for nearly nothing other than, of course, great creative rewards. He also spent a long time talking about comedy and the then-unknown Richard Curtis and Rowan Atkinson. He and Eric have done it the hard way. I love their willingness to champion unconventional filmmakers. They take risks and they bet on talent even though I know for a fact that this high-wire act scares them more than they would ever admit. Think of all of the talent whose big breaks came through Working Title. Besides Curtis and Atkinson, they were the ones who bet on Hugh Grant, Stephen Daldry, Roger Michell, Mike Newell, Shekhar Kapur and many others. Tim, Eric, Liza, Debra and I have a lot of war stories between us, from the highs of *Billy Elliot*, *Notting Hill*, and *About a Boy* to a few lows which keep us all humble. If only this book were for our eyes only, then I could share a few behind-the-scenes tales. The problem is they all involve clients who would probably leave me as a result.
**– Beth Swofford, Agent, CAA**

**Sharon Maguire, Hugh Grant and Eric Fellner discuss a scene**

# JOHN MADDEN
Director, *Captain Corelli's Mandolin*

I was a late arrival in the Working Title family, and something of an interloper, too.

*Captain Corelli's Mandolin* had been a project of Working Title's since Kevin Loader and Roger Michell brought the book to them some time before it became the literary phenomenon of the 1990s. A protracted process of getting the movie set up had resulted in an amber light in September 1999 when Nic Cage agreed to play Corelli; the light turned greenish just as a medical emergency threatened Roger's ability to continue. Following his sudden incapacitation, Kevin and Tim Bevan asked me to step in. I didn't know the material at that point, but two-and-a-half readings of the book, two-and-a-half meetings with Shawn Slovo, and an utterly disarming exhortation from Roger were enough to put me under the spell, and I entered a tunnel from which I was not to emerge until nearly two years later, and then into a hailstorm.

The critical reaction notwithstanding, the film remains an extraordinarily special experience for everyone involved with it. The way in which making a film can reflect the story it is telling is a phenomenon familiar to anyone in the business, but I have never found it to this degree. A foreign, though benign, force arrives to occupy a beautiful island – its motives and intentions the subject of deepest suspicion. It sets up encampments and workshops, and offers work and reassurance to its hosts. It helps to build towns and villages (and then destroys them), and doubtless many Pelagias find many Corellis. Over time, the suspicion transforms, miraculously, into something else – a mutual bond of affection and respect, and a gratitude on the part of the island that their experience is being acknowledged and communicated. When the time comes to return home, no one wants to leave.

It was a hard lesson to learn when the film came out, that my own intentions with it were the subject of deep suspicion as well: the suspicion that we had invaded and colonized something beautiful and true, and cosmeticized and traduced a great book in the service of an ingratiating Hollywood orthodoxy. To be misunderstood on such a huge scale is painful, and in those circumstances it matters hugely that you are not fighting your corner alone. In fact, every taste the film has left is a sweet one, and much of that is due to the support and loyalty of Tim and Eric, and that unmistakeable feeling we all had that it was the work and the experience that counted. Though in another demonstration of Working Title's nose for what its audience wants to see, the film performed extremely well in the UK (if disappointingly in the US, and somewhere in-between everywhere else).

I went back to Cephallonia for a holiday a year after the film's release. Hugs and emotional reunions aside, it felt exactly the way it had when we first went to scout it. The only trace of our presence was the renaming of two bars: you could drink at Captain Corelli's in Sami or Agia Ephemia. The much-talked-about surge in tourism materialized, then subsided, registering with it minimal significance on the Richter scale. There was something immensely reassuring about this. The island had healed itself again, but it had not forgotten.

I first met Tim and Eric on *Plunkett & Macleane*, before producing alongside them on *Captain Corelli's Mandolin*, *Johnny English* and *Thunderbirds*. All three films have presented us with different challenges but none fractious enough to ruin the relationship. *Corelli*, shot entirely on location in Cephallonia, was a logistical challenge. Not only did we have to ship all the military vehicles over from Europe, we had crew from the UK, Italy and of course Greece. Islands may be idyllic holiday destinations but for a film it can bring about an overabundance of problems. Apart from all this, John Madden had the unenviable task of transferring a hugely successful book to the screen, which in my opinion he achieved with his usual grace and talent.
**– Mark Huffam, Producer**

*Opposite:* **Director John Madden in conversation with Nicolas Cage on the set of *Captain Corelli's Mandolin***

# KEVIN LOADER
## Producer, *Captain Corelli's Mandolin*

Maybe the most extraordinary thing about *Captain Corelli's Mandolin* is that it ever got made at all. Tim Bevan had been keeping encouraging tabs on both Roger Michell and me since we'd made Hanif Kureishi's *The Buddha of Suburbia* for the BBC in 1992. Two years later, when I read Louis de Bernières' extraordinary novel and gave it to Roger, we knew two things: firstly, it had the potential to be a fabulous film, and secondly, that Working Title were the only people worth approaching with it. Who else could combine Hollywood resources with enough non-Hollywood cultural ambition to share our vision? After all, the story contains no American or British characters, and is a brilliant – and very European – examination of how people's differences are never as important as what they have in common. It's to Tim's great credit that he never wavered from his initial passion after he'd read the book over a weekend and immediately decided to share the vision. All films take years to reach the screen, and *Corelli* hit the average – six. Few have to deal with not only a corporate convulsion, in the transfer of Working Title from PolyGram to Universal, but also the preferred star's reluctant withdrawal from the project (though thankfully Nic Cage returned to us again when his domestic situation eased), and then the trauma of the original director retiring hurt during pre-production.

Apart from his trademark power naps, I still don't understand when John Madden found time to sleep from the moment he took creative charge of the film in mid-December 1999, until the moment we left Cephallonia at the end of the following August. By the time I first talked to John about the film, I had spent much of the previous two years visiting Greece, tried to master basic Greek, had a design team simultaneously surveying locations in two Ionian islands, and a major star financially contracted to shoot the film in a matter of months. John handled this unimaginable pressure with his customary grace and amazing focus – and maintained both until the film was finally completed, eighteen months later.

The privilege of living and working on that spectacular Greek island has now become an ever-changing compendium of magical memories: Penélope Cruz stepping off the plane from Athens with a newly adopted stray cat in a holdall; Paul Englishby, our musical director, recording the operatic excerpts with our Italian actors in a flower-filled field behind the rehearsal rooms; the cathedral-like hush that descended over the baking heat of the set for two days when we shot the terrible firing squad scenes in a deserted village that had probably witnessed the original events; the black smoke of the battle scenes cloaking the town of Sami while the locals crowded on the rooftops, hoping to catch a glimpse of Nicolas Cage finally wielding an automatic weapon. Above all, we all left with new friendships, a huge respect and gratitude for our Greek hosts, and a pledge to return as soon and as often as possible.

Roger, Tim, John and I had always been convinced that Nic was the right actor for the part – who else could have combined the complex mix of qualities that Louis' leading character required? For some reason, the critics couldn't get past the baggage they thought he brought to the part, which was narrow-minded of them and heart-breakingly frustrating for us. Thankfully, audiences don't pay much attention to critics. My hope is that Nic's performance, and John's direction, will find their deserved place in the critical canon long after the spurious and ill-informed sniping about 'Hollywood's cultural imperialism' has been forgotten.

*Opposite:* **Pelagia (Penélope Cruz) and Captain Corelli (Nicolas Cage) embrace passionately in** *Captain Corelli's Mandolin*

**Pelagia (Penélope Cruz) dances with an Italian Soldier (Nunzio Lombardo) in *Captain Corelli's Mandolin***

I'm thrilled to be part of this magic scene, which defined an important moment of the whole movie. This image captures the result of a period of intense and exciting rehearsal time with Penélope and the Italian soldiers. It was a great pleasure working in such a wonderful production; having the chance to learn how to put the passion of acting, into action.

**– Nunzio Lombardo, Actor**

# RICHARD CONWAY
Special Effects Supervisor, *Captain Corelli's Mandolin*

For *Captain Corelli's Mandolin* we were pleased to provide the physical effects for so great a story, filmed in its correct historical location. Our main commitment was obviously going to be the crushing of Italian troops by the German forces, and its dire consequences. There had recently been released some excellent Second World War films, with gritty highly credible action. One was *The Thin Red Line*, photographed by John Toll, who was to be Corelli's photographer. Although I was repeatedly reminded this was not a war story, I knew our work had to be peerless.

The battle action was to be staged in the coastal resort of Sami, a functioning seaport, with the necessary quays for the docking of the film's warships. The film's period town set was built around the existing seafront shops, bars and hotels of the port. It was in this set that we filmed the battle sequence. Shooting over several days, we staged some fairly substantial explosions, almost continuous gunfire and perpetual grey smoke. As evening arrived, we'd visit the adjacent bars fully expecting to be rebuked for the hell we'd initiated throughout the day, but the locals thought it great fun.

We needed to stage the exploding of a beached mine, the chosen location featured amongst the planet's seven most beautiful beaches and the bay was home to a protected turtle population. I sought out the local environmentalists and explained how we would achieve the impression of total devastation, with minimal impact. The director's brief was a huge explosion, which we achieved and, with a couple of hours clear-up, the beach was still in the top seven and the turtles in blissful repose.

# JIM CLAY
Production Designer, *Captain Corelli's Mandolin*

Ten years on from *A Kiss Before Dying*, on the Greek island of Cephallonia, we take over the holiday town of Sami and go to work. The fine Italianate town square needs to provide an architectural world as beautiful and humane as the landscape we are to build in, if I am to provide the sharpest of contrasts to the barbaric events which took place on this island over four days in the summer of 1943. Six months later we are shooting the battle for Argostoli. Tourists sip their gin and tonics on the other side of our set while we fill the air with explosions, gunfire and acrid smoke. Now there is no evidence that we were ever there, except for the renaming of local bars and the postcards of 'Old Cephallonia' which enterprising locals produced from stolen photos of our set.

**The Battle for Argostoli: Cinematographer John Toll checks his light meter on the set of *Captain Corelli's Mandolin***

In 1999, PolyGram changed ownership to Universal Pictures and Working Title maintained its style of producing special scripts outside of mainstream filmmaking. Double Negative continued to work with Working Title, overseeing the visual effects for the epic love story *Captain Corelli's Mandolin* directed by John Madden. Shot on the beautiful island of Cephallonia, Paul Riddle supervised the visual effects for the Second World War set pieces. For practical and compositional reasons all the flying 'Stukas' were digital creations, allowing the freedom for more handheld camera work during the battles. The director, in post-production, was able to place the fighter planes into whatever part of the scene he chose.
**– Peter Chiang,
Visual Effects Supervisor**

*Overleaf:* **Mandras (Christian Bale) throws Pelagia (Penélope Cruz) into the clear blue waters of the Ionian Sea**

**Ed Crane (Billy Bob Thornton, left) and Frank (Michael Badalucco) take time out from their barber duties**

**Relaxing on the set of *The Man Who Wasn't There***
Billy Bob Thornton (left) lists the ingredients for the 'Arkansas Stew' prepared that morning in his trailer. Ethan Coen had tried a bowl; Eric Fellner had abstained.
**– Ethan Coen, Filmmaker**

*Opposite:* **Director Joel Coen and Ed Crane (Billy Bob Thornton) in the Barber Shop**
Joel Coen and Billy Bob Thornton try to work out which end of the broom to hold.
**– Ethan Coen, Filmmaker**

**Doris Crane (Frances McDormand) puts on her stockings with Cinematographer Roger Deakins (right) and First Assistant Cameraman Andy Harris, in attendance on the set of *The Man Who Wasn't There***
I really enjoyed doing this insert with Deakins. It was just my foot for God's sake – but it was in a period blue stocking. We collaborated on just the right arch and angle – the speed and smoothness of the stocking pull. I said 'Roger, is this boring you?' His reply 'No, I could do this all day'.
**– Frances McDormand, Actress**

**Frances McDormand with Hairdresser Paul LeBlanc**
Monsieur LeBlanc – the man for period hairstyles and wig work. We met on *Mississippi Burning* and Paul has worked with Joel and Ethan many times. They truly appreciate his talents. *The Barber* movie (aka *The Man Who Wasn't There*) was a joy for Monsieur LeBlanc because of the cuts and dos.
**– Frances McDormand, Actress**

**Big Dave Brewster (James Gandolfini, centre) practises strangling Ed Crane (Billy Bob Thornton) under the eagle eye of Roger Deakins (second left)**

**Ed Crane (Billy Bob Thornton) and Doris Crane (Frances McDormand) each in a world of their own in *The Man Who Wasn't There***

Scary scenario. Marriage gone sour. After we wrapped *The Man…* I told Billy I hoped to work with him some day. That's how unconnected the two characters were to each other.
**– Frances McDormand, Actress**

# PAUL WEITZ
Writer & Director (with Chris Weitz), *About a Boy*

As an American, I was a bit apprehensive about coming to London to adapt *About a Boy* into a film. But there were two things that set me at ease. The first one was my discovery that British people spoke English. That really was a load off my mind – I wouldn't have to learn a new language!

The second thing that put me at my ease was that we were working with Working Title. My first meeting was with Tim Bevan in Los Angeles. It was on the set of a Revlon ad shoot – Tim had just been made the 'face' of Revlon's new cosmetics line for men. Tim graciously took time to speak to us in the midst of his rigorous modelling. He gave us his savvy opinion on script, suggested crew, and asked us, 'Wouldn't we rather have Richard Curtis write and direct this?'. We asked Tim Bevan, 'But then what would we do?'. 'Think about it', he said, picking up a pair of nunchuks and whipping them round his body.

We met Eric Fellner soon after arriving in London. An old-school charmer, he took us to the Ivy and gave us script notes, and offered to have male prostitutes sent up to our hotel room. After haggling over the bill with the waiter (Eric claimed he had asked for only a half-order of chips), Eric said he had a brilliant idea: 'What if Richard Curtis wrote and directed the movie!'.

In the months to come, we saw a great producer in action. Eric was great with actors. He had a special relationship with our star, Hugh Grant, often standing behind Hugh, waving for our attention, and making circling 'he's crazy' gestures with his index finger. He was terrific with Nick Hoult, the eleven-year-old actor who played Marcus. 'Do a good job,' Eric would say, 'or I will destroy you in the business'. 'Learn how to act!', he would growl at Toni Collette, often in the middle of a take. He insisted on personally applying Rachel Weisz's make-up, and would burst into tears at the slightest criticism, such as, 'Eric, you got lipstick all over her face'. 'You try to make this horse look pretty!', he would sob, and then stalk off the set.

He was assiduous in trying to track down the millions of dollars that seemed to disappear from our shooting budget, often making special trips to the Cayman Islands to try and follow the paper trail. 'Don't you worry your little heads about it,' he would laughingly say. 'Or I'll have you shot'.

We were now part of the Working Title family, Eric told us, which meant we could wash his Ferrari on weekends. But the thing that made us really feel at home was when Eric would allow us to trim his seven-day growth of beard back down to five days' growth. 'At least you're good for something', he would say with a smile. 'Not even Richard Curtis is as good a barber as you guys are'.

**Directors' chairs on the set of *About a Boy***

**Producer Eric Fellner (left), Writer/Director Paul Weitz (centre) and Writer/Director Chris Weitz on set**

*About a Boy* was another wonderful experience for us all. Working on a good story with good actors and something new to me, two directors. The Weitz Brothers were determined to make a very good film and were equally determined to make the process a joy for everyone involved. Hard work really can be fun. Shekhar, on *Elizabeth* had his ritual breaking open and sharing of a coconut after the first take of each day. The brothers Paul and Chris did twenty push-ups each time we put a new roll on the camera. They co-directed very smoothly and all discussions were done with both brothers. They would check each other's ideas and could bounce ideas around without worrying about offending themselves as they were brothers. They came fully loaded with some unusual ideas like starting a camera move before the shot begins. We got on very well, meeting every Saturday to talk through the next week's scenes.
**– Remi Adefarasin, Cinematographer**

*Opposite:* **Marcus (Nicholas Hoult, left) and Will (Hugh Grant) on a day out at London Zoo in *About a Boy***
The ease of conversation, eh! Looks like we're having fun! My family got to be extras that day.
**– Nicholas Hoult, Actor**

**Marcus (Nicholas Hoult, right) and Will (Hugh Grant) outside Rachel's house in *About a Boy***
Here we are on the doorstep of the lovely Rachel Weisz's house in the film, (for anybody who was about to try and track her down).
**– Nicholas Hoult, Actor**

*Below:* **Will (Hugh Grant) and Marcus (Nicholas Hoult) on stage during the school concert**
Now here's my co-star making a complete wally of himself, it was so satisfying! The king of cool being uncool, the rooster being the chicken, the spider being the fly.
**– Nicholas Hoult, Actor**

*Opposite, above left:* **Hugh Grant and Nick Hornby on set**
This is Hugh Grant on the set of *About A Boy*, trying to persuade me that he could play the role of a feckless, wealthy, resolutely single and faintly lecherous man in his mid-to-late thirties. I didn't get it at first. But he managed to convince us all.
**– Nick Hornby, Author**

*Opposite, above right:* **Hugh Grant, Writer/Director Paul Weitz (seated), Cinematographer, Remi Adefarasin (standing) and Producer Nicky Kentish-Barnes study the monitor during filming**
*About a Boy* was a delightful film to make. I was always a fan of the book and the screenplay did justice to the book. Paul and Chris Weitz were great directors to work with and they took their job very seriously yet demanded a sense of fun on the set. Hugh too was a joy to be near and he gave a remarkable performance. Nicholas Hoult was another joy to watch.
**– Remi Adefarasin, Cinematographer**

*Opposite, below:* **On the set of *About a Boy*: Hugh Grant watches himself on the playback monitor. Other cast and crew members share the moment**

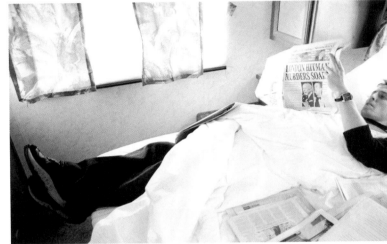

# NICK ANGEL
Music Supervisor, Working Title Films

The idea for a slight less traditional way of choosing a composer originated from Paul and Chris Weitz, who had been listening to the Badly Drawn Boy album 'The Hour Of Bewilderbeast' whilst working on the script. They wanted the score to relate to the film in the same way that Simon and Garfunkel's music did for *The Graduate*. An idea, incidentally, that had also occurred to Nick Hornby.

We invited Damon down on set for a meeting in a double-decker bus with Paul and Chris, Eric Fellner, Nicky Kentish Barnes and Hugh Grant. He had read the book instead of the script and had already written his first idea which turned out to be 'Something to Talk About', the first single.

We split his work into two camps. Tom Rothrock (Beck, Foo Fighters) produced the songs and Steve McLaughlin (Gohl/McLaughlin – a great soundtrack producer) worked with Damon on all the incidental music and adapting the themes from the songs into being themes for the movie.

One of the things that happens with film, which has no correlation with the music business, is the idea of testing films. Paul and Chris didn't want to 'temp' the film with other movies' music, as they wanted to reflect what eventually Badly Drawn Boy would deliver. This gave us a few hairy moments as some very important screenings for some very important people had scratchy demos and random tracks chosen from his first album covering some very key scenes. Never attempt to temp a film with demos if you can avoid it, because in front of 300 people or so on a giant screen, knowing how it is *going* to sound is no substitute to how it *actually* sounds! However, the line was held and when the music was delivered everybody was thrilled, and thus a very unique score was created.

This film is quoted back to me many times, by record companies, managers, etc., as something their artists could do and I would like to think, with the complexion of Working Title as it is, this is an experiment we would do again.

*Opposite, above left:*
**A contemplative Toni Collette on the set of *About a Boy***

*Opposite, above right:*
**Hugh Grant in Make-up on the set of *About a Boy***
Eric Fellner in wig applies Hugh Grant's make-up.
**– Paul Weitz, Writer/Director**

*Opposite, centre right:*
**Hugh Grant relaxing in his Winnebago on the set of *About a Boy***

*Opposite, below:*
**On the set of *About a Boy***
Paul Weitz (left), Rachel Weisz and Chris Weitz try to understand something Eric Fellner has said.
**– Paul Weitz, Writer/Director**

*Left:* **Artwork for the Badly Drawn Boy soundtrack for *About a Boy***

**Erica Sutton (Shannyn Sossamon) and Matt (Josh Hartnett) on the set of *40 Days and 40 Nights***
I couldn't just give Josh a big hug here like I wanted to 'cause I would've messed up the measuring – so instead I pretended to fix his hair.
**– Shannyn Sossamon, Actress**

# MICHAEL LEHMANN
## Director, *40 Days and 40 Nights*

When producer Michael London, writer Rob Perez, and myself were looking for a studio to support the development of *40 Days and 40 Nights*, my agent suggested we take the idea to Working Title. Rob's idea for a movie about a young man who gives up all things sexual for Lent was a tricky one to pitch: on the one hand, the concept for the movie could be easily encapsulated and simply told, which is a good thing when talking directly to a Hollywood studio; on the other hand, we had aspirations to make a more intelligent version of this idea, which would likely be a detriment in the studio world. Since the people at Working Title had a history of commercial success with intelligent movies, we hoped they would appreciate a somewhat unconventional approach to what might otherwise be very conventional material.

Liza Chasin was our first contact with Working Title, and she stayed heavily involved throughout the making and release of the movie. But Tim Bevan also happened to be in Los Angeles the week we brought the idea to Working Title, so my first meeting on the project was with Tim. He struck me as thoughtful, articulate, with a good sense of humour; he also clearly understood what kind of movie we wanted to make and seemed to support that. He impressed me with his ability to make a quick decision: within a couple of days, he'd bought the pitch and we put Rob to work.

Over the following months, with Liza handling the details and day-to-day of development, Tim stayed involved, reading drafts of the script and offering notes, and Working Title confirmed their reputation as a company with strong creative support of their filmmakers. Because Rob delivered a good first draft and Liza stayed so close to the process, and because she and Tim communicated so well, we had a relatively smooth time developing the script.

Working Title has a reputation as a filmmaker-driven filmmaker-supportive company. That's unusual in the world of major studio filmmaking. It's unusual, even, in the world of independent films these days, as the success of 'small' movies in the big marketplace has raised the stakes for producers and attracted people whose money interests far outweigh their creative interests. Tim and Eric, I thought, would be mostly 'hands off', and I expected a high degree of independence in the shooting and editing of the movie.

**Outside the Laundromat: Erica (Shannyn Sossamon) and Matt (Josh Hartnett) flirt with one another in *40 Days and 40 Nights***

During the making of *40 Days*, I was struck by how 'hands-on' Working Title were. At first, I was surprised and concerned: if these guys are so filmmaker-friendly, then why do they stay so closely involved? Why don't they just leave me alone and let me make the movie? I've had a long career manoeuvering the minefields of studio production (you might call it 'dependent filmmaking') with only partial success, so I can be a bit prickly when it comes to these things. But what I found, to my happy surprise, was that Tim presented himself as collaborative while being extremely supportive. By keeping him involved, I had the benefit of his opinions, which were consistently intelligent, and the benefit of his support. On those (rare) occasions where we disagreed, he never pushed his point of view without backing it up, and he never, ever, forced me to do anything I didn't agree with. This was an unexpected and very satisfying situation. I finally learned that the best situation isn't one in which you are left alone as a filmmaker; it's better to have intelligent collaborators who can support your vision and contribute to making a better movie.

Before working with Working Title, I'd never shown a rough 'work in progress' edit of a movie to the producers until I had time to work the material to my satisfaction. Michael London, the producer who developed the movie, brought it to Working Title with me, and who remained my closest collaborator on the film, told me halfway through shooting that Tim was going to be visiting the set and wanted to see a rough cut. I was in a panic, nervous that the cut wasn't ready to be seen, and I was very resistant, but Michael reassured me that Tim and Liza were only being supportive. They needed, he said, to know what they were supporting if they were going to be supportive. In the heat of the battles that happen in film production, in an arena that is driven more by marketing than art, when the dollar stakes are high, the forces that pull you in different directions can easily destroy a film. Clearly, one of the many reasons Working Title has had so much success is that they establish trusting relationships with filmmakers and have a good sense of when it's important to step in and when it's important to step back.

Throughout the editing and release of *40 Days*, Tim Bevan and Liza Chasin provided creative input on the rough cuts and worked diligently with the studio to protect the interests of the film. I always felt that *40 Days* was a bit of a departure for Working Title because, at the end of the day, it is at heart an American youth comedy. But from the beginning to the end, Tim and Liza supported our movie as strongly as any of their others; I cannot imagine a better situation for a filmmaker.

**Director Michael Lehmann with Liza Chasin, President of Production US, Working Title Films, on the set of *40 Days and 40 Nights***
Our exhausted expressions and the green screen in the background show me that this was taken on the last day of production. We were shooting flying shots of Josh Hartnett that day on a cold Vancouver effects stage. And it's a great sign that after over forty days and nights of shooting, Liza and I were still smiling!
**– Michael Lehmann, Director**

# DAISY VON SCHERLER MAYER
Director, *The Guru*

## Excerpts from Daisy Mayer's diary

**21 March 2000**… Spoke with Tom at agency, looking good to direct wacky astronaut comedy!… Wacky astronaut comedy?… Wanted to be important filmmaker…

**27 March**… New script! *The Guru of Sex*. Indian actor comes to N.Y. ends up charlatan sex guru. All about yoga (new aerobics) and spirituality. Have been meaning to get inner life! Best part: fab musical numbers! Must get film!

**12 April**… Interview with Liza Chasin at Working Title, love her, cool leather trousers and raunchy talk about Beverly Hills women taking blow-job classes (see *Esquire* article).

**20 April**… Met writer, Tracey Jackson, really into yoga and spirituality (had that Gwyneth $1,500 handbag). Said she wrote *Guru* for important filmmaker Shekhar Kapur but he's unavailable since Oscar® hit *Elizabeth*. Am obvious next choice!

**2 May**… Interview with Tim Bevan (big Kahuna at Working Title) raunchy humour not a hit with massively reserved Brit male. He asked me what I'd like people to learn from the film, I said, sex tips. Dead silence. Have lost film with fab musical numbers.

**11 July**… YEAA! Got film! Feel like singing and dancing! But don't know how… in fact know nothing about musicals, just have a lot of gay friends. Am screwed.

**20 December** (London)… No 'green light' from studio re: revised script, light 'blinking amber'. Met super-sexy *East is East* guy, Jimi Mistry. Serious actor. Wonder how he'd look in leather trousers? Glam dinner with Heather Graham, really into yoga and spirituality, discussed Tantric sex. Must find out what Tantric sex is, something to do with Sting (am only familiar with tantrum sex).

**14 March**… Light 'blinking green'! Blink due to budget issues. Working Title suggested cutting fab musical numbers but agreed to keep them in exchange for my first born. Celebrated by sending super-serious Brainiac assistant to rent porn for 'research'… crew loved this!

**13 April**… Start filming Monday. Producer friend says make first day easy to impress bosses with speed. Oops. Am starting with much-maligned difficult musical number.

**16 April**… YEAA! *Bridget Jones's Diary* is gi-normous boffo box-office hit! Zillions and zillions of dollars! Pounds! Whatever! Tim Bevan, visiting on set, can't stop smiling (must have points in *Bridget*) tapping his feet to the music! He loves fab musical number! Everyone does! Send Renée Zellweger thank you note? No, can't keep doing that.

**26 April**… Jimi Mistry drops trousers! WHAT A TALENT!

**7 May**… New best friend, Marisa Tomei (really into yoga and spirituality!) wants better lingerie for Scene 56 (something about deepening her character too). Lingerie very important as we must show off her incredible ass! Probably comes from yoga. Or spirituality? Must ask her.

**11 May**… Jimi's pregnant wife is here and about to burst. Must be a way to deliver baby on day off. Can studio schedule Caesarean birth? No, that's crazy… Talk to legal.

*Opposite, above:* **Sharonna (Heather Graham) and Ramu Gupta (Jimi Mistry) share a wedding kiss in *The Guru***

*Opposite, below:* **From Bollywood to Hollywood Sharonna (Heather Graham) shows off her Bollywood dance moves in *The Guru***

**On the set of *The Guru*:
Director Daisy von Scherler
Mayer listens intently to 'super-
sexy' actor Jimi Mistry whilst
Tim Bevan the 'big Kahuna at
Working Title' listens in**

**21 May**… Baby born on day off! Without legal intervention! Gods love film! Parents love baby! Jimi wants day off! Talk to legal.

**24 May**… Thirty-seven shots in one day (multiple camera) on actual set of *Sally Jesse Rafael* show. Jimi so tired at 5a.m. he could barely stand, totally lost Indian accent. Must re-record as he slurred unintelligibly like Billy Idol.

**28 May**… No time to write. Twenty-hour days then endless drive home from dangerous outer boroughs with Brainiac driving (am saving money on extra Teamster) and me watching for random gunfire. Paul Weitz called from *About a Boy* set. Just to chat. Which he has time to do. They shoot eight-hour days then go to the Bristol for a pint with Eric and Hugh. Try and work for Eric next time.

**4 June**… Am all about challenges! 'Stole' scene in Times Square; no lights, no security, few crew, finished before theatres let out and fat tourists recognized Heather – am kick-ass director chick! Can't wait for India!

**23 June** (Old Delhi, India)… Dizzy with heat stroke, stomach ill, never seen such crowds (not even Barney's clearance sale)… set can only be reached by bicycle rickshaw. John De Borman, portly cinematographer, insists we share rickshaw seat and talk shot list… can't concentrate, eyes glued on ninety-pound cyclist, he's about to drop dead, no, I am… and for what?… what's the point… why…

**ONE YEAR LATER**

**20 August, 2002**… Wore fab purple sari to huge London premiere, like exotic princess (but white). *The Guru* (studio thought *of Sex* would alienate Iowa) opened number one! Big boffo box-office hit! Like *Bridget*! (well, not quite). Material success not important since epiphany in India (better to be in rickshaw than driving it). Being important filmmaker not important either. Am really into yoga and spirituality (and have better ass!).

# MICHELLE WRIGHT AND SARAH-JANE WRIGHT
Head of Production and Production Executive, Working Title Films

### Production in the 2000s

**MW:** For me the challenge coming to the UK (from the US) in 1999 was to bridge the gap between an independent production company and the corporate side of things – to convince the corporate world of Universal that we can make films with both tremendous European and American talent and still do it for a price. Tim and Eric have given us a tremendous amount of autonomy both with the studio, and in the day to day running of things. We aren't the ones who usually give good news – we are the ones who say 'you can't do this, and you can't do that'. It's about finding the right balance between the movie 'business' and the very creative aspects of the film making process.

**SJW:** You never know what's going to happen – the project you think is least likely is often the one that comes from nowhere, so we are constantly trying to anticipate which movie will go first. We are lucky with the production crews we have worked with constantly over the years, both in the UK and the US. All extremely talented people whose careers we have watched and who now make sure they are available to us when our films come along. Our jobs are made easier because we can work with people that we know so well and trust implicitly. We also have the rewarding factor of watching people we have placed on training schemes rise through the ranks and become talented crew members in their own right.

**SJW:** From the production point of view, the work now is incredibly varied and to work in the production department means that you are dealing with a picture that costs $3 million in the morning and a picture that costs $60 million in the afternoon – but you have to give each film your undivided attention. Since 2000, we have gone up a gear in terms of the number of films we are making and the scope of those films. It's been a steep learning curve, but there is nowhere else in the UK that one can get this experience.

**MW:** In reverse, for me, there is no where else I can get the experience on the *Billy Elliot*'s of this world.

**SJW:** We also have an enormous amount of fun doing this – we laugh a lot.

**Jimi Mistry and Heather Graham rehearse the wedding celebration scene in *The Guru* under the watchful eye of Director Daisy von Scherler Mayer (far left)**

**Booyakasha!**
**Ali G (Sacha Baron Cohen)**

*Opposite:* **The glasses, the hat, the bling bling jewellery! Inside Ali G's dressing room. Sacha Baron Cohen is reflected in the mirror**

# NATASCHA WHARTON & RACHAEL PRIOR
Head of WT² & Head of Development, WT²

### Humour, Horror, Heart – WT²

We announced the advent of WT² at the Cannes Film Festival in 1999 and almost overnight were inundated with scripts. We were delighted and terrified by the response… We started building our slate up, and by the beginning of 2000 we were lucky enough to be shooting *Billy Elliot*, WT²'s first feature. In 2001 we were invited back to Cannes with the film, which played to hugely enthusiastic crowds as part of Directors Fortnight.

From the moment everyone from the company crammed into a tiny office at Working Title to watch the first rushes of Jamie Bell dancing on the roof and down the street, we knew there was something special about this particular film. But it wasn't until we started screening the actual film to Working Title staff, most of whom emerged from the screening theatre in tears, that we realised the impact the film might have. In Cannes the audience erupted into spontaneous applause during one of Billy's dancing scenes – it was such an incredible and unexpected reaction and a fantastic experience for everyone who had worked on the film. Jamie Bell hadn't ever flown before, and he was suddenly surrounded by all the attention, press and glamour of Cannes. Yet he handled everything with such maturity, and seemed the least fazed of everyone.

As we set about turning our attentions to the next WT² productions, Tim and Eric told us in no uncertain terms (and with a certain amount of glee) that we would have to operate as they did back in the early days of Working Title – in other words, like independent producers, scrimping and saving, pulling in favours. When they set the budget on *The Calcium Kid*, at $2.5 million, it felt like a huge challenge. They would constantly refer back to *Four Weddings and a Funeral* (shot over six weeks on a shoestring) or further back to *Sid and Nancy* and *My Beautiful Laundrette* – 'We bore the pain of low-budget filmmaking. Now it's your turn!'

Luckily the crew on *Calcium Kid* had a fantastic sense of camaraderie. It was a much smaller team than you would find of on a bigger budget movie, and so there was an intimacy that made for an enjoyable work environment. Budget constraints meant that the all the departments had to be very creative with how they spent their money. When the Production Designer was complimented on a brilliant seventies-style swirly carpet on one set, he confessed it had been found the night before in a skip by an art department trainee, fresh out of art school.

WT² still follows the same philosophy it set out with: to make commercial movies, with exciting new talent on lower budgets. According to Tim Bevan, WT² is about "humour, horror and heart" and our recent production *Shaun of the Dead*, a Rom Zom Com (as the director so aptly describes it) seems to fit this description quite uncannily.

**Shaggy (right) and Ali G (Sacha Baron Cohen) on the set of their video shoot 'Me Julie', from the *Ali G Indahouse* soundtrack**

*Centre:* **Ali G (Sacha Baron Cohen) and his friends from the Massives set a new trend for multi-coloured combat gear in *Ali G Indahouse***

On the first day of filming *Ali G Indahouse* in South Central LA, the first AD made an announcement, saying, 'We are in a very dangerous part of town, we're firing guns, just so you are aware, someone might mistake this for a real situation, be very careful'. It was funny, but secretly we Brits were nervous. Sacha (Baron Cohen) was confronted by actual ex-gang members, hired by an extras agency who specialize in helping guys like these off the streets and back into the community. The night before we did the shoot, the armourer asked, 'Has anyone here handled a gun before?' to which everyone except Sacha put up their hand. Some of the extras had to take fake bullet shots, so the armourer then asked if 'anyone had ever seen anyone get shot?'. Again, they all put up their hands. If Sacha was scared, he never confessed to it. It was Sacha who had pleaded for us to go to LA to shoot this opening sequence, so we kept saying to the director, Mark Mylod, 'Make sure there is a bloody palm tree in shot! Something to show that we really are in LA given how much it's cost to get here!'.
– **Natascha Wharton, Head of WT² and Rachael Prior, Head of Development, WT²**

**On location for *Ali G Indahouse* in South Central LA. Producer Natascha Wharton (left), Ali G (Sacha Baron Cohen) and Director Mark Mylod try to keep in with the locals whilst shooting in LA**

## PETER HOWITT
Director, *Johnny English*

The most testing challenge of creating the *Johnny English* film was to take a character that had only ever been called upon to be funny and interesting for a minute at a time and keep him alive and dynamic in a story lasting an hour and a half. To flesh out a character that had been created purely to sell something, was a hard task.

Although I came into the development process after a year or so, it was immediately apparent to me that the first port of call were the adverts themselves. They were shot in a rich and sophisticated manner – short films more than simply adverts. But the character still needed extra layers. You may think, having watched Rowan Atkinson make us laugh for years, that as long as it's funny, credibility has no place at the comedy dining table. Nothing could be further from the truth. Every successful comedy character we have enjoyed over the years has had very specific foibles, likes and dislikes and, most importantly, self-serving agendas. What makes us laugh is seeing them constantly fail to realize these agendas. This is where *Johnny English* slightly differed from the formula. Although he is the first to congratulate himself, usually just that crucial ten yards before the finish line, this is not what drives him. He is driven by duty. Because he is a hero it was important that the audience rooted for him to succeed. So each scene and sequence had to be crafted quite carefully in order to encourage the audience to enjoy his misjudgements, *but* to continue to want him to get up and ultimately finish the job. This is the area that Rowan and I found the most demanding and I was surprised how little difference there is in creating a comedy character from a straight one.

When I was at Drama School in 1976, the head of the school, Peter Layton, proudly announced before a term break: 'Next term, the serious business of comedy'.

What a smart arse he turned out to be!

*Opposite:* **Director Peter Howitt watches the playback monitor on the set of *Johnny English***

*Left to right:* **On the set of *Johnny English:* Johnny English (Rowan Atkinson) takes a break; Director Peter Howitt (right) shows Rowan Atkinson to make a gun with his hands; Johnny English (Rowan Atkinson) with 'gun'**

# DAVID APPLEBY
## Still photographer, *Johnny English*

It was a real thrill to be offered *Johnny English*, a chance to meet and work with Rowan Atkinson and see the comic genius perform in the flesh – not literally, there were no nude scenes planned, after all it's a film for all ages. Also the chance to photograph Natalie Imbruglia, and that turned out to be the easiest job of all, my camera loved her. I couldn't go wrong, she just looked great in every photo.

One of the biggest thrills, though, was working once again with the great John Malkovich after a gap of nineteen years. It was on John's first movie, *The Killing Fields,* that we first met. We all felt then that this boy was going to be good; we were certainly right. John was a delight, he was still the down-to-earth, gentle, hard-working professional; fame hadn't changed him one bit.

As a still photographer on movies, one of the most important things is to try and create still images that truly represent a movie and capture the essence of the characters. Comedy can be difficult, I didn't want to end up with just a selection of funny expressions, those may work for Mr Bean but they wouldn't work for Johnny English. Johnny English is a serious secret agent, dedicated to his work for Queen and country, suddenly thrown into the deep end with rapid promotion. He takes his job very seriously, it's just that when things happen to him they create very funny comic situations and all the time he tries to retain his dignity. There is a little of Johnny English in all of us, so it's possible to identify with him. Rowan looks great in a serious 'James Bond' pose. It's just because it is Rowan that you know that something unusual is going to happen. I hope I've managed to achieve what I set out to do.

*Johnny English* is a very glamourous and lavish production and for a British comedy I haven't seen anything as good-looking since the *Pink Panther* movies.

There were two other very special projects that I was involved with in the early years of Working Title. *A World Apart,* which reunited me with double Oscar®-winning cinematographer Chris Menges in his director debut, after working with him on both *The Killing Fields* and *The Mission. A World Apart* was a fine movie that carried a very anti-apartheid message that we all believed in. Also *Hidden Agenda* and the opportunity to work with Britain's greatest filmmaker, Ken Loach. A film that gave me a really much deeper insight into the issues and problems of Northern Ireland, again a very important film and all credit for getting this message to the screen.

**John Malkovich between scenes with Eric Fellner on the set of *Johnny English***

*Johnny English* – starring the iconic Rowan Atkinson whose performances I have enjoyed since his days in *Not the Nine O'Clock News* – was a wonderful film to be part of. With a script written by the team behind the last two Bond movies, Neal Purvis and Rob Wade, the ever-inventive Will Davies and of course, Rowan's crucial perception of the character, the script developed into a very British comedy. With Peter Howitt at the helm, and a fantastic crew that included Chris Seagers, Paul Jennings and Adam Somner, I feel that *Johnny English* fulfilled all Working Title's expectations and satisfied audiences.
**– Mark Huffam,
Producer *Johnny English***

*Opposite:* **Natalie Imbruglia studies her call sheet on the set of *Johnny English***

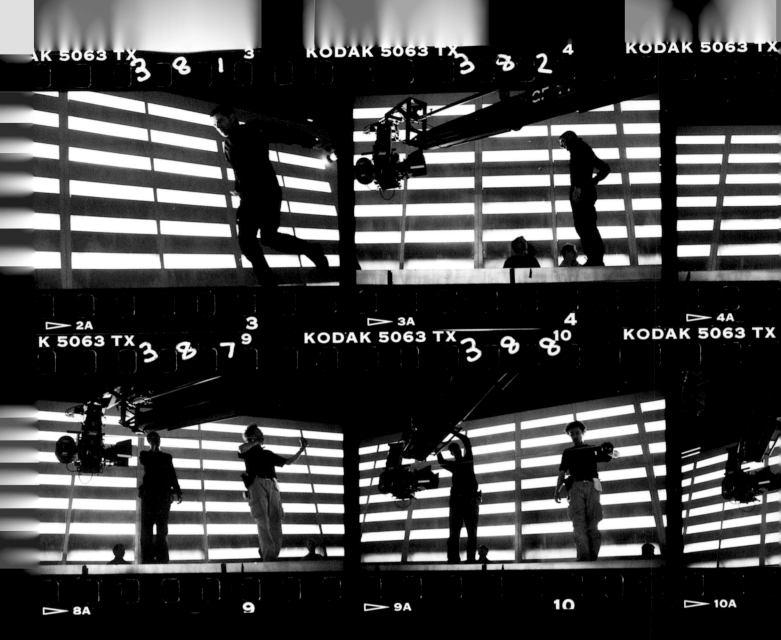

*Johnny English* was my second collaboration with Peter Howitt. This was a comedy blessed with the loveliest of actors, Rowan Atkinson. The script was totally re-worked after the destruction of the World Trade Center in New York. Peter and I flew to South Africa on that fateful day and we both realized not only was our script going to change but the world was changing too. The shoot was delayed for months and instead of shooting in South Africa, the South of France, Thailand and Russia, we found ourselves in Shepperton Studios and locations in London. Despite the upheavals, we all had a good time making the film and tried to make the most of the Englishness.
**– Remi Adefarasin, Cinematographer**

## LIZA CHASIN
President of Production US, Working Title Films

### The day the world changed

We're developing a script called *The Interpreter*. We're in New York to tour the United Nations. It's the last morning of our trip. We're at The Four Seasons. The message light is flashing. It's Tim. We're not going to LA. Turn on your television. I run through the hallways in a state of new found terror. Tim opens his door. I cry. We stand on the 47th floor staring at the television, trying to figure out what to do. Get. Out. Of. The. Building. Pedestrians are everywhere. The only sounds, the whirr of sirens… all headed in the same direction. Downtown. We see a cloud of smoke at the end of lower 5th Avenue. We keep walking towards Central Park. A cell phone call tells us that the first tower has fallen. The smoke turns downtown into darkness. People just keep walking uptown. The sirens keep whirring. The park begins to fill. Small groups form around boomboxes blaring the news. We stand

*Johnny English* action sequence

and listen. The second tower falls. Our hearts are pounding. We sit on a bench. The sirens continue to wail and the sky now buzzes with fighter jets. Movies are the last thing on our minds, though it feels like we're in one. The cell phones don't work. Eric e-mails me on my Blackberry. I am so happy to hear from him.

When developing scripts, we often talk about the 'you-have-to-bring-the-audience-down-to-remind-them-how-much-fun-the-up-is' moment. You need the 'Funerals' to earn the 'Weddings'. I am happy to say that my twelve years of working with Tim and Eric have consisted of far more 'Weddings' than 'Funerals' and I'm happy to have weathered and

**Rowan Atkinson in make-up on the set of *Johnny English***

*Right:* ***Johnny English* stunt shot over Canary Wharf**

In 2002, I was second unit director on *Johnny English* as well as Visual Effects Supervisor. The use of visual effects enabled me to present sequences to the director and producers before a single frame of film had been shot. This allowed for aesthetic appraisal of the shots as well as providing all necessary technical information to all the other departments working on the film. For example, the complicated car chase in the film was storyboarded, then pre-visualized in the computer to obtain the lens information and the vehicles' speed and distance covered. Similarly a parachute sequence was broken down to determine which shots would be live-action on set with Rowan Atkinson, which would feature stunt performers against a green screen, and which would be live in a helicopter flying over London at night.
**– Peter Chiang,
Visual Effects Supervisor**

# ROBERT WADE & NEAL PURVIS
Writers

As writers, we have noticed Tim and Eric have different approaches to script development: a) Perhaps we could re-work that ten or twenty times? (Eric method.) b) Ah fuck it… (Tim method.) Back in the mists of a non-existent British film industry, Tim was a towering beacon of hope to young writers – he had a photocopying machine. While pretending to subsidize our writing by coming up with ideas for pop promos (£100 a pop) for Tim's video outfit, Aldabra, we were secretly using the Xerox to run off copies of our first screenplay.

Shortly after that (and for some reason, neither Tim nor Eric seem able or willing to remember this) we wrote the very first combined commission for them, well before they joined forces in Working Title. It was an adaptation of a music-biz novel by Tony Parsons, which they can't have believed was all that hot – or they'd surely have let us actually read the book.

This was most inauspicious. It could have derailed what went on to be an enormously talented and hugely successful partnership. But enough about us. Suffice to say the film never got made but it seems Tim and Eric realized they could work together and the consequence has been woeful for anyone else in the British film industry releasing a film in the same week as them…

*The thing with Tim?*
The thing with Tim is that you know there is absolutely no chance of creative compromise – so long as you're prepared to be sacked for your beliefs. He once got us in a room with Rowan Atkinson. We had just written the Bond movie *The World is Not Enough* (Tim had been kind enough to not not put in a good word for us when asked by producer Barbara Broccoli), and Tim and Rowan were contemplating a movie based on his Barclaycard character. We said there were only two problems: 'We don't do Bond spoofs and we don't do spin-offs from ads'. Tim sniffed, put the tape of the Bond-spoof ads in the video, and three years later, *Johnny English* came out.

*And Eric?*
Like most writers in England (and indeed, in the whole world), we have developed quite a few scripts with Working Title, but the only other one to have emerged with our names on it was *Plunkett & Macleane*. It may not have been Shakespeare, but for us it was definitely a filmic tragedy. Eric's habitually courageous experimental approach to script development (which is often very successful, especially when practised by the Coen brothers) unfortunately started to go wrong for us. There was only one thing to do – fire the writers. But nicely. No shouting.

This lack of shouting was counterbalanced when Tim exploded because we were working on two jobs simultaneously (both for him) and he only wanted us to work on one. But Eric apologized for Tim's behaviour and Tim apologized for Eric firing us on *Plunkett* (Tim was possibly drunk). All in all, a well-balanced partnership, then – based on a mastery of one simple technique: the meting out of tiny disarming moments of kindness – fleeting glimpses of humanity – to keep one in line.

There are so many examples, one could go on and on (like their partnership)… But as Tim would say, fuck it.

**The Kelly Gang ride out across
the Australian Bush**

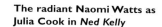

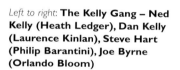

**The radiant Naomi Watts as Julia Cook in *Ned Kelly***

*Left to right:* **The Kelly Gang – Ned Kelly (Heath Ledger), Dan Kelly (Laurence Kinlan), Steve Hart (Philip Barantini), Joe Byrne (Orlando Bloom)**

*Below left:* **Supt Hare (Geoffrey Rush) on the path of Ned Kelly**

*Below centre:* **Hair and Make-up Designer Jenny Shircore puts the final touches to Geoffrey Rush's beard on the set of *Ned Kelly***

*Below right:* **Joe Byrne (Orlando Bloom) and Ned Kelly (Heath Ledger)**
*Ned Kelly* Director Gregor Jordan knew Orlando Bloom was his Joe Byrne the first time he read for us in London.
**– Jina Jay, Casting Director**

**The Final Shootout in *Ned Kelly***

*Opposite:* **Setting up a village scene**

*Below left:* **Oliver Stapleton (left), Director Gregor Jordan (centre) and Heath Ledger on the set**
As I got used to working with Gregor, his precise framing ideas grew on me. Looks like I can't wait to get the viewfinder back in this photo!
**– Oliver Stapleton, Cinematographer**

*Below right:* **Heath Ledger and Naomi Watts watch themselves on the playback monitor during filming**

**Billy Mack (Bill Nighy, centre)
and the Christmas Girls in *Love
Actually***

# RICHARD CURTIS
Writer and Director, *Love Actually*

*Love Actually* **is the first film you've directed. How was it?**
I now consider Mel Smith, Roger Michell and Mike Newell to be saints. It must have been unbelievably difficult having me around – directing a film is complicated, and the director is always making little compromises in his mind, thinking, 'Well I can't do this because of time, or because of how the actor is, or because of the location, and that'll be fine – I'm going to get almost everything I want'. But I wasn't even allowing them to make those sorts of compromises – I would always be standing behind, saying, 'But don't you remember we said seven months ago, that she was going to be hitting a different emphasis in that sentence?'.

**The film is actually lots of stories, isn't it?**
Yes – and credit to Working Title for not saying, 'Please don't risk this one.' There was never a quibble from Eric or Tim at any point, or anyone from Universal, telling me not to try. Because I could probably have written something much more commercial – the movie actually contains two or maybe three whole, easier movies. I was going to write the one about a prime minister falling in love with one of his staff, and had also mapped out one about someone falling in love with a girl who doesn't speak the same language as him. But once again, when I decided on trying the multi-story thing, Tim and Eric said, 'Fine, if that's what you want to do, have a go'. That repeated saying – 'have a go' – that's one of the reasons why it's so easy to carry on working with the company.

**Have you been bitten by the directing bug?**
Not really. I don't think I'd ever direct anything I hadn't written because I think they would be hiring, in Mike Newell's words, a 'pig in a poke'. But maybe I will direct things I write in future – though, there are some things I'm thinking of writing, for which I may not be the most apt director. We'll see. Or maybe after this one I'll not be asked to work again. Tim and Eric are, after all, ruthless, unprincipled bastards.

**'Directing a film is complicated…'
Richard Curtis on location in
Marseille**

**The *Love Actually* read through:**
*Below left, left to right:* **Martine McCutcheon, Liam Neeson, Thomas Sangster, Colin Firth and Lucia Moniz** *Below right, left to right:* **Emma Thompson, Hugh Grant, Martine McCutcheon and Liam Neeson**

**Aurelia (Lucia Moniz) chases her employer's wind-strewn story pages into the lake in *Love Actually***

In Terry Gilliam's *Brazil*, de Niro's character is attacked by wind-borne litter, which attaches itself to his body, progressively engulfing him into a ball of paper, rolling off to his fate. There was nothing so gruesome in *Love Actually*, but that experience with controlling wind-blown sheets of paper helped in the scene where the Colin Firth character realizes he is in love with his Portuguese housekeeper. His love is aroused when she strips and dives to retrieve his story pages, blown from the table at which he was typing, into a lake at his French farmhouse. This could be achieved digitally, but no way would it look as natural, and hell, where's the fun in that!

**– Richard Conway, Special Effects Supervisor, *Love Actually***

**Chris Newman (left with clapperboard) stays dry whilst Aurelia (Lucia Moniz) gets wet on location in France.**

I've learnt that limitless optimism and dogged determination are the vital elements for surviving an unpredictable industry, which can equally reward with strange and sublime experiences. Just take a particular week's work on Richard Curtis's *Love Actually*. One day in Kenya working amongst the Masai warriors, building a set in the bush, while their chief showed off his new i-Pod. Three days later – London, overseeing the stills shoot for a Christmas pornographic photographic exhibition – surrounded by naked models with festively shaved pubic hair, casually drinking tea and exchanging the smallest of talk between takes. The next day we have a meeting with a rather more discreetly attired Gordon Brown who took Richard and myself on a guided tour of the inner sanctums of Downing St, including a glimpse of Margaret Thatcher's bathroom. There stands an old cast iron bath dominated by a large wall clock with an enormous revolving 'second' hand relentlessly reminding you that it's always later than you think.

**– Jim Clay, Production Designer**
*Love Actually*

*Opposite: clockwise from above left:*
**On the set of *Love Actually*: Mark (Andrew Lincoln) professes his love for Juliet; Juliet (Keira Knightley) gets ready for her wedding; Hugh Grant (left), Richard Curtis (centre) and Martine McCutcheon (right) discuss a scene; Daniel (Liam Neeson) and Sam (Thomas Sangster) between takes; Karen (Emma Thompson) takes a break; Martine McCutcheon does a dance for Richard Curtis**

*This page: anti-clockwise from below:*
**Writer/Director Richard Curtis deep in thought; The Prime Minister (Hugh Grant) dances at No 10; On the set of *Love Actually*; Harry (Alan Rickman); Writer/Director Richard Curtis (seated) and Duncan Kenworthy (standing)**
This is the apartment where Mark (Andrew Lincoln) lives and stores pictures from his art gallery. Just out of shot is the TV on which Juliet (Keira Knightley) has watched his video of her wedding and found out how much he loves her. Richard and I are either moved to silence, or speechless at how long the filming's taking.
**– Duncan Kenworthy, Producer**

**Lady Penelope (Sophia Myles) and Parker (Ron Cook) outside Buckingham Palace in *Thunderbirds***

When I first heard we were getting in business with a company called 'Working Title', I said, 'Tell them to come back when they have a real title'. Who in the world names a company 'Working Title?'. In the film business it means, temporary, transient, to be replaced by something permanent. Well, after twenty years there is nothing temporary or transient about Working Title or Tim and Eric and I am honored to have been a part of their 'Working Title' for the last twelve of those years.
**– Rick Finkelstein, Executive Vice-President, PolyGram Filmed Entertainment 1994-99; President and COO, Universal Pictures 2001 – present**

# WILLIAM OSBORNE
Screenwriter, *Thunderbirds*

During my time as a screenwriter I've enjoyed/suffered some interesting challenges. I won't forget in a hurry having to write sixty new pages of script over one wet (yes, wet) weekend in a Los Angeles hotel room. But even on that Richter scale of writing, being asked to reinvent the cult children's TV show *Thunderbirds* commencing in December 2001, so that it could be greenlit by the studio before the rights expired at the end of 2002, still constituted for me 'the big one'. It also proved to be one of the most rewarding of my career, the only time I have had a big-budget, special-effects-heavy film taken from 120 blank pages to production in less than one year. And that is in no small measure due to the professionalism, integrity and tremendous support I was given by Tim Bevan, Eric Fellner and Working Title's development team, not to mention the amazing visual effects department and storyboard artists. I thank you all.

The film is currently in post-production and won't be in cinemas until 2004 so, like all films at this stage, we await the finished product. For those who don't know the old show, it centred around a family called the Tracys, five adult brothers and their widowed father living on an island hideaway which housed fantastic futuristic rescue vehicles which comprised International Rescue. We knew we had to reposition the movie for a wider family audience, so I decided to focus the story on the youngest brother, now a teenager, and two other kids living on the island. For the most part, I felt the story should take place on the island itself, shades of *Treasure Island* but also drawing on the Western tradition of protecting the homestead from the bad guys. We all like to be scared a little in these films but we also like

to laugh, so humour was a vital ingredient in the development of the screenplay. Hopefully Lady Penelope and her trusty chauffeur, Parker, provide plenty of this!

Then, of course, there were the fantastic machines. I fully appreciated that the film was being seen as a possible franchise with all the marketing and platform opportunities that entails. I made every effort to feature them as 'characters' in the story, while also trying to use as many of them as I could, without it becoming a case of – cue another amazing vehicle!

I completed a number of drafts over the spring and summer of 2002, which the studio batted back across the ocean with their notes. And slowly the finished script took shape, first and third acts changing the most, to accommodate creative, budget and production imperatives. So the collapse of the Golden Gate Bridge during the day at the opening of the story became a rescue from a burning oil rig at night. A final action sequence in Geneva was relocated to London and the villain, after a number of incarnations, finally became the Hood from the original TV series (sensitivities to portraying an Eastern villain on screen having eased since the calamity of 9/11).

When the green light came in September 2002, I was, of course, pleased for myself but also for Working Title. Pleased, but also a little sad, because, as a screenwriter on these sort of projects, when that moment is reached our job is in effect over and the whole thing starts its countdown before it blasts off. I wish it *bon voyage*, or as the Thunderbirds would say, F.A.B.

**Parker (Ron Cook) holds the door of FAB 1 open for Lady Penelope (Sophia Myles) in *Thunderbirds***

Six o'clock on a beautiful Sunday morning, dressed in a made-to-measure silver-grey chauffeur's uniform. Driving Sophia Myles down the Mall to Buckingham Palace in a twenty-eight-foot, six-wheeled pink, FAB 1. One of the most enjoyable jobs I have ever had.

**– Ron Cook, Actor**

# EPILOGUE ERIC FELLNER

Concorde… memorable and important in the life of this film producer… technically, creatively and financially an international monolith with major brand awareness, and then… gone.

A salutary tale that cannot be dismissed. You can ride high, and even touch the stars (metaphorically and physically), yet still gravity – or reality, call it what you will – will ultimately win out. Pessimistic? Perhaps. But success is illusory, however tangible it may seem.

We work in a world where endeavour is paramount and our emotional psyche is dictated by the level of success one has just enjoyed. In the fast moving and slate-driven business we find ourselves in today though, success is something we crave yet can't enjoy. As my partner Tim taught me many years ago, if you hang around basking in the glory, your business soon turns to mud, slippery and ultimately useless to build on. One, two, even three years can go by until your next project sucks oxygen… so don't enjoy, don't luxuriate, move on, keep moving and don't take no for an answer; that's what I've learnt – and it has taken twenty years.

Reading the contributions in this book, and looking at the photographs from the last twenty years I am struck by what an amazing thing Tim and Sarah did all those years ago in setting up not only a film company, but one with the truly great name 'Working Title'. With and without my involvement it has brought employment to thousands, and the realisation of dreams to hundreds.

Today it is totally a sum of all its parts – be they the creative executives in London, Los Angeles and Sydney, the business people, the production people, the money creatures, the marketing and distribution guys, and all the other committed and talented members of our staff. It sounds pat, but they truly are the reason Working Title is able to consistently produce five or so films a year, and those who know this business know that five films is a lot of work.

There are other things that strike me: the sheer diversity of the work, from *A World Apart* to *Bean* and back to *Fargo* and on to *Notting Hill* and then *Elizabeth* to *Posse* and back to *O Brother, Where Art Thou?*. This year alone brings us zombies (*Shaun of the Dead*), tennis (*Wimbledon*), *Thunderbirds*, *Bridget Jones* (again) and the powerful teen drama *Thirteen*. This ability to make high and low-budget films, both specialist and genre films, is a rare and wonderful thing: rare because it is difficult to find constant worldwide distribution for films that are this varied; and wonderful because it feeds one's soul yet at the same time  allows us to have a realistic and positive business plan.

On top of this we have been blessed with our corporate partners… firstly PolyGram, and now Universal. Both have been believers in the company, and have trusted us enough to let us get on with it, with only a minimum of second guessing. If this is a place for thanks, then thanks must go to Michael Kuhn and his entire team for teaching us how to walk and to believe that 'commercial', 'hit' and 'British' were three words that could co-exist. And now to Stacey Snider and Ron Meyer and their entire team for supporting us and introducing us to the studio system and all that it brings.

In trying to identify the magic ingredient, it is glaringly obvious… talent. And here again we have been extraordinarily lucky. We have worked with the greatest writers, directors, actors and technicians. In the early days at Initial Films, at Working Title and WT², and both in the

I didn't realize that Tim does most of the decision making and Eric really has very little, if anything at all to do with, well… anything regarding Working Title Films… and he always seems so busy. Interesting. Being Bridget Jones was the most challenging, all encompassing exercise in loneliness management that I have ever been happy to be part of. I love Bridget Jones. While I'm at it I'd like to thank Eric properly for all of it. Thanks, Eric.
**– Renée Zellweger, Actress**

*Opposite:* **Eric Fellner and Renée Zellweger between takes on the set of *Bridget Jones's Diary***

*Above right to left:* **Anna Scott (Julia Roberts) and Max (Tim McInnerny) dance at her wedding in a deleted scene from** *Notting Hill;* **Joel and Ethan Coen in New York**
During the video press kit for '*The Man Who Wasn't There*', Joel Coen (left) encourages the interviewer to humour brother Ethan who describes his first sighting of a UFO; Ethan still insists the movie was heavily autobiographical.
**– Ethan Coen, Filmmaker**

*Below left to right:* **Eric Fellner and Hugh Grant on the set of** *About a Boy;* **Walter Sobchak (John Goodman) and The Dude (Jeff Bridges) between takes on the set of** *The Big Lebowski*

UK and the US; these people are our lifeblood and I hope that we will continue to make many more films with the creative partners we already have.

As I look to the future, I see a British film business in a similar state to when I joined it. The names are different, the financing entities are different, but the potential is still there. A thriving list of young actors, some already established in the world wide arena; a growing number of aspiring directors working alongside many well established names; but sadly still not enough producers working at a truly entrepreneurial level. The lifeblood of any industry is its risk takers, and we don't seem to have enough. The business is an international one and we have to be prepared to travel – for money, distribution, ideas and talent. By remaining insular in an international world we will pay the price of marginalisation. Our revenues are a small percentage of the world market and as such we will always be a cottage industry, but we must strive to ensure that we are a thriving one, not a dying one.

As such I think the future has to include an enormous amount of resources put into training programmes. Not only the crafts, but also into the work of generating the roles of

producer, writer and director. We must implore those that have the funds, to spend them in this direction. If only more DNA films, Fragile Films, SKA Films or Civilian Contents were to appear, then we would be making more films, developing more opportunities and starting more careers. With inward investment of time as well as money, surely this will be possible.

In closing this remarkable chapter of the Working Title story I, like Tim, am struck by the amazingly varied films we have been involved in and how we have collaborated with the most incredibly talented people. Between us all we have generated lasting memories, $2.5 billion at the box office and not least some wonderful films.

With a lot of luck and even more hard work we will hopefully not fall prey to market forces and become outdated before our time. Due to the demise of Concorde we will travel a little slower, which who knows, might be better for us… but we will still end up getting there.

Thanks go to everyone who has ever been involved in any way on all of our movies.

*Above left to right:* **Eric Fellner and Gary Oldman on the set of *Sid and Nancy*; Richard Curtis directs Emma Thompson in *Love Actually***

*Below right to left:* **Jamie Bell dances his way to stardom in *Billy Elliot*; Sacha Baron Cohen and Director Mark Mylod rehearse on the set of *Ali G Indahouse*;**
This is Sacha and me saluting the national anthem traditionally played each morning before the first set-up.
**– Mark Mylod, Director,**

## HUGH GRANT
Actor

**Eleven things you never knew about Tim Bevan and Eric Fellner**

**Tim**

**1.** He is from New Zealand.
**2.** He is known as the sheep-shagger.
**3.** He seldom speaks.
**4.** That's it.

**Eric**

**1.** He is Dutch.
**2.** He has a startlingly bendy golf swing, like one of those pipe cleaner men on *Vision On*. Or the beginning of a dream sequence.
**3.** He will buy anything you try to sell him, so long as it's expensive.
**4.** He has very poor balance. Every few weeks he tumbles heavily from his skis or his motorbike.
**5.** His left shoulder blade is made of metal, and makes a 'ting' sound if you rap it sharply with a putter.
**6.** If you buy an exciting new car and are waiting six months for it to be delivered, he will buy an identical second hand one in the interim, drive it for two weeks and declare it 'disappointing'.
**7.** I once told Stacey Snider (President of Universal) that she would be machine-gunned if she didn't have sexual intercourse with either Tim or Eric. She didn't like it but went for Eric.

**Hugh Grant (left) plants an affectionate kiss on Eric Fellner's cheek on the set of *Bridget Jones's Diary***

# MIKE NEWELL
*Director, Four Weddings and a Funeral*

I can't remember a time when Working Title wasn't a fact of life. I don't think many people think of it as 'Working Title'. It's TIM-N-ERIC. I've always been impressed by their offices. You would think that Tim was the style-queen slob and Eric the 'a place for everything and everything in its place' machine man. And it's the other way around. So who is the good cop and who the bad? I've never known. Perhaps that's one of the secrets of their phenomenal success. They are also very good at doing two other things. One is flying the Atlantic (if you ever look out in mid-air and see another plane passing you at 30,000 feet over Greenland, it's a good bet that one of them is on it). And the other area of expertise they share is going on holiday at exactly the time you don't want them to.

In every sense they made my fortune. And I also love them for themselves alone.

(Is this enough? If you don't like it say anything you want. Please send more money.)

Love,

MIKE

*Left to right:* **It's a Wrap! Writer Richard Curtis, Producer Duncan Kenworthy and Director Mike Newell on the set of *Four Weddings and a Funeral***

## SIMON WRIGHT
President, WTTV

It would be nice to say that WTTV have played their part in the success of Working Title – but it's not really true. Not that Tim and Eric have not been good to me and WTTV. After three years working at their offices I finally got a desk. Although it was six more months before the chair arrived.

There always seems to have been a space issue at Working Title. The more altruistic put this down to the popularity of the company, with so many people wanting to work for it. I have heard – from the bitter and twisted, of course – that they cram everyone in small offices so that they can listen through the walls.

In 1999 WTTV set up a satellite office. WTTV had doubled its size – to two. I know, though, that they haven't forgotten about us up at mission control. Tim nods to me, every Christmas, when we attend their party. As for Eric, I've never actually met him and I'm pretty sure he has no idea who I am. I hear, however, he's a very nice man.

Finally, I have been known from time to time, at parties, to take credit for producing etc. some of Working Title's bigger successes. For the record:

**1.** I did not produce *Four Weddings and a Funeral*.
**2.** *Fargo* was not my idea.
**3.** It wasn't because of my relationship with Julia Roberts that she agreed to do *Notting Hill*.

*Left to right:* **Tim Bevan, Angela Morrison (COO, Working Title Films), Debra Hayward (Head of Film, Working Title Films UK), Natascha Wharton (Head of WT²) and Eric Fellner. Simon Wright was not invited to be in this picture...**

*Opposite:* **The Millennium Bridge: a scene from *Love Actually***

*Overleaf:* **The illusion stripped bare: on *Elizabeth*, technicians and crew set up the Night Regatta scene, in the tank at Shepperton studios**

# FILMOGRAPHY

**My Beautiful Laundrette** (1985)
**Director:** Stephen Frears. **Writer:** Hanif Kureishi.
**Producers:** Tim Bevan, Sarah Radclyffe.
**Cinematographer:** Oliver Stapleton. **Music:**
Stanley Myers, Hans Zimmer. **Cast:** Saeed Jaffrey,
Roshan Seth, Daniel Day-Lewis, Gordon Warnecke,
Shirley Anne Field.

**Caravaggio** (1986) A BFI Production.
**Director:** Derek Jarman. **Writer:** Derek Jarman.
**Producer:** Sarah Radclyffe. **Costume:** Sandy
Powell. **Cast:** Tilda Swinton, Dexter Fletcher, Robbie
Coltrane, Sean Bean.

**Personal Services** (1986)
A British Screen/Zenith Co-Production. **Director:**
Terry Jones. **Writer:** David Leland. **Producer:** Tim
Bevan. **Cinematographer:** Roger Deakins. **Cast:**
Julie Walters, Alec McCowen.

**Wish You Were Here** (1987)
A Channel 4/Zenith Co-Production
**Director:** David Leland. **Writer:** David Leland.
**Producer:** Sarah Radclyffe. **Cinematographer:**
Ian Wilson. **Music:** Stanley Myers. **Cast:** Emily Lloyd,
Tom Bell

**Sammy and Rosie Get Laid** (1987)
**Director:** Stephen Frears. **Writer:** Hanif Kureishi.
**Producers:** Tim Bevan, Sarah Radclyffe.
**Cinematographer:** Oliver Stapleton. **Music:**
Stanley Myers. **Editor:** Mick Audsley. **Cast:** Shashi
Kapoor, Frances Barber, Claire Bloom, Roland Gift.

**A World Apart** (1988)
**Director:** Chris Menges. **Writer:** Shawn Slovo.
**Producer:** Sarah Radclyffe. **Exec. Producers:** Tim
Bevan, Graham Bradstreet. **Cinematographer:** Peter
Biziou. **Music:** Hans Zimmer. **Cast:** Jodhi May, Jeroen
Krabbé, Barbara Hershey, Tim Roth, Linda Mvusi.

**Paperhouse** (1987)
**Director:** Bernard Rose. **Writer:** Matthew Jacobs.
**Producers:** Tim Bevan, Sarah Radclyffe.
**Co-producer:** Jane Frazer. **Music:** Stanley Myers,
Hans Zimmer. **Production Design:** Gemma
Jackson. **Make-up:** Jenny Shircore. **Cast:** Charlotte
Burke, Glenne Headly, Ben Cross.

**For Queen and Country** (1988)
**Director:** Martin Stellman. **Writers:** Martin
Stellman, Trix Worrell. **Producer:** Tim Bevan.
**Cinematographer:** Richard Greatrex. **Costume:**
Sandy Powell. **Cast:** Denzel Washington.

**The Tall Guy** (1989)
**Director:** Mel Smith. **Writer:** Richard Curtis.
**Producer:** Tim Bevan. **Cinematographer:** Adrian
Biddle. **Cast:** Jeff Goldblum, Rowan Atkinson,
Emma Thompson.

**Diamond Skulls** (1989)
**Director:** Nick Broomfield. **Writer:** Tim Rose-
Price. **Producer:** Tim Bevan. **Cinematographer:**
Michael Coulter. **Music:** Hans Zimmer. **Cast:**
Gabriel Byrne, Amanda Donohoe.

**Chicago Joe and The Showgirl** (1989)
**Director:** Bernard Rose. **Writer:** David Yallop.
**Producer:** Tim Bevan. **Cinematographer:** Mike
Southon. **Music:** Hans Zimmer. **Production Design:**
Gemma Jackson. **Cast:** Kiefer Sutherland, Emily Lloyd.

**Fools Of Fortune** (1990)
**Director:** Pat O'Connor. **Writer:** Michael Hirst
(based on book by William Trevor). **Producer:**
Sarah Radclyffe. **Exec. Producers:** Tim Bevan,
Graham Bradstreet. **Music:** Hans Zimmer. **Cast:** Iain
Glen, Mary Elizabeth Mastrantonio, Julie Christie.

**Dakota Road** (1990)
**Director:** Nick Ward. **Writer:** Nick Ward.
**Producer:** Donna Grey. **Exec. Producer:** Sarah
Radclyffe. **Cast:** David Bamber, Amelda Brown.

**Drop Dead Fred** (1991)
**Director:** Ate de Jong. **Writer:** Elizabeth
Livingston (story), Carlos Davis, Anthony Fingleton.
**Producer:** Paul Webster. **Exec. Producer:** Tim
Bevan. **Cast:** Phoebe Cates, Rik Mayall.

**Rubin and Ed** (1992)
**Director:** Trent Harris. **Writer:** Trent Harris.
**Producer:** Paul Webster. **Cast:** Crispin Glover.

**Edward II** (1991)
**Director:** Derek Jarman. **Writers:** Ken Butler,
Steve Clark-Hall, Derek Jarman (after play by
Marlowe). **Producers:** Steve Clark-Hall, Antony
Root. **Exec. Producer:** Sarah Radclyffe. **Costume:**
Sandy Powell. **Cast:** Steven Waddington, Andrew
Tiernan, Tilda Swinton.

**Robin Hood** (1991)
Produced for 20th Century-Fox
**Director:** John Irvin. **Writers:** Sam Resnick, John
McGrath. **Producers:** Tim Bevan, Sarah Radclyffe.
**Cast:** Patrick Bergin, Jürgen Prochnow, Uma
Thurman, Jeroen Krabbé.

**London Kills Me** (1991)
**Director:** Hanif Kureishi. **Writer:** Hanif Kureishi.
**Producers:** Tim Bevan, Graham Bradstreet. **Cast:**
Justin Chadwick, Steven Mackintosh, Roshan Seth,
Fiona Shaw, Brad Dourif.

**Bob Roberts** (1992)
**Director:** Tim Robbins. **Writer:** Tim Robbins.
**Producer:** Forrest Murray. **Exec. Producers:** Tim
Bevan, Ronna B Wallace, Paul Webster.
**Cinematographer:** Jean Lepine. **Cast:** Tim Robbins,
Alan Rickman, Gore Vidal, James Spader, Helen Hunt ,
Susan Sarandon, Peter Gallagher, John Cusack.

**Map Of The Human Heart** (1992)
**Director:** Vincent Ward. **Writer:** Louis Nowra.
**Producers:** Tim Bevan, Vincent Ward. **Exec.
Producers:** Bob & Harvey Weinstein, Graham
Bradstreet. **Co-Producer:** Tim White. **Music:**
Gabriel Yared. **Production Design:** John Beard.
**Cast:** Jason Scott Lee, Anne Parillaud, Patrick Bergin,
John Cusack, Jeanne Moreau.

**The Young Americans** (1993)
**Director:** Danny Cannon. **Writers:** Danny
Cannon, David Hilton. **Producers:** Alison Owen,
Paul Trijbits. **Music:** David Arnold, Björk. **Cast:**
Harvey Keitel, Iain Glen, Keith Allen, Thandie
Newton, Viggo Mortensen.

**Romeo is Bleeding** (1994)
**Director:** Peter Medak. **Writer:** Hilary Henkin.
**Producers:** Hilary Henkin, Paul Webster. **Exec.
Producers:** Tim Bevan, Eric Fellner. **Cast:** Gary
Oldman, Lena Olin, Annabella Sciorra, Juliette Lewis.

**Posse** (1993)
**Director:** Mario Van Peebles. **Writers:** Sy
Richardson, Dario Scardapone. **Producers:** Preston
Holmes, Jim Steele. **Exec. Producers:** Tim Bevan,
Eric Fellner. **Co-Producer:** Paul Webster. **Cast:**
Mario Van Peebles, Stephen Baldwin, Billy Zane,
Melvin Van Peebles.

**The Hudsucker Proxy** (1994)
**Director:** Joel Coen. **Writers:** Ethan Coen, Joel Coen, Sam Raimi. **Producer:** Ethan Coen.
**Exec. Producers:** Tim Bevan, Eric Fellner.
**Cinematographer:** Roger Deakins. **Music:** Carter Burwell. **Cast:** Tim Robbins, Jennifer Jason Leigh, Paul Newman.

**Four Weddings and a Funeral** (1994)
**Director:** Mike Newell. **Writer:** Richard Curtis.
**Producer:** Duncan Kenworthy. **Exec. Producers:** Tim Bevan, Eric Fellner. **Cinematographer:** Michael Coulter. **Production Design:** Maggie Gray.
**Costume:** Lindy Hemming. **Music:** Richard Rodney Bennett. **Cast:** Hugh Grant, Andie MacDowell, Kristin Scott Thomas, Simon Callow, John Hannah, James Fleet, Charlotte Coleman.

**That Eye, The Sky** (1994)
**Director:** John Ruane. **Writers:** Jim Barton, John Ruane, Tim Winton. **Producers:** Grainne Marmion, Peter Beilby. **Exec. Producers:** Tim Bevan, Fred Schepisi. **Cast:** Peter Coyote, Lisa Harrow.

**Panther** (1995)
**Director:** Mario Van Peebles. **Writer:** Melvin Van Peebles **Producers:** Mario Van Peebles, Melvin Van Peebles, Preston Holmes. **Exec. Producers:** Tim Bevan, Eric Fellner. **Cast:** Kadeem Hardison, Bokeem Woodbine, Joe Don Baker, Courtney B Vance, Angela Bassett.

**French Kiss** (1995)
**Director:** Lawrence Kasdan. **Writer:** Adam Brooks. **Producers:** Tim Bevan, Eric Fellner, Kathryn F. Galan, Meg Ryan. **Exec. Producer:** Charles Okun.
**Production Design:** Jon Hutman. **Costume:** Joanna Johnston. **Cast:** Meg Ryan, Kevin Kline, Timothy Hutton, Jean Reno.

**Moonlight and Valentino** (1995)
**Director:** David Anspaugh. **Writer:** Ellen Simon.
**Producers:** Tim Bevan, Eric Fellner, Alison Owen.
**Cinematography:** Julio Macat. **Music:** Howard Shore. **Cast:** Elizabeth Perkins, Whoopi Goldberg, Gwyneth Paltrow, Kathleen Turner, Jon Bon Jovi.

**Loch Ness** (1995)
**Director:** John Henderson. **Writer:** John Fusco.
**Producers:** Tim Bevan, Eric Fellner, Steve Ujlaki.
**Music:** Trevor Jones. **Cast:** Ted Danson, Joely Richardson, Ian Holm.

**Dead Man Walking** (1995)
**Director:** Tim Robbins. **Writer:** Tim Robbins (based on book by Sister Helen Prejean CS).
**Producers:** Tim Robbins, Jon Kilik, Rudd Simmons.
**Exec. Producers** Tim Bevan, Eric Fellner.
**Cinematography:** Roger Deakins. **Music:** Nusrat Fateh Ali Khan, Bruce Springsteen, David Robbins.
**Cast:** Susan Sarandon, Sean Penn.

**Fargo** (1996)
**Director:** Joel Coen. **Writers:** Joel Coen and Ethan Coen. **Producer:** Ethan Coen.
**Exec. Producers:** Tim Bevan, Eric Fellner.
**Cinematographer:** Roger Deakins. **Production Design:** Rick Henrichs. **Music:** Carter Burwell.
**Editor:** Roderick Jaynes. **Cast:** Frances McDormand, William H. Macy, Steve Buscemi, Peter Stormare.

**The Matchmaker** (1997)
**Director:** Mark Joffe. **Writers:** Greg Dinner, Karen Janszen, Louis Nowra, Graham Linehan. **Producers:** Tim Bevan, Eric Fellner, Luc Roeg. **Co-Producers:** Liza Chasin, Debra Hayward. **Cast:** Janeane Garofalo, David O'Hara , Denis Leary.

**Bean** (1997)
**Director:** Mel Smith. **Writers:** Richard Curtis, Robin Driscoll. **Producers:** Peter Bennett-Jones ,Tim Bevan, Eric Fellner. **Co-Producer:** Rebecca O'Brien.
**Music:** Howard Goodall. **Cast:** Rowan Atkinson, Peter MacNicol, Burt Reynolds.

**The Borrowers** (1997)
**Director:** Peter Hewitt. **Writers:** John Kamps, Gavin Scott (based on books by Mary Norton).
**Producers:** Tim Bevan, Eric Fellner, Rachel Talalay.
**Co-Producers:** Liza Chasin, Debra Hayward.
**Production Design:** Gemma Jackson. **Cast:** John Goodman, Jim Broadbent, Mark Williams, Celia Imrie, Hugh Laurie.

**The Big Lebowski** (1998)
**Director:** Joel Coen. **Writers:** Joel Coen and Ethan Coen. **Producer:** Ethan Coen.
**Exec. Producers:** Tim Bevan, Eric Fellner.
**Cinematography:** Roger Deakins. **Music:** Carter Burwell. **Cast:** Jeff Bridges, John Goodman, Julianne Moore, Steve Buscemi, Philip Seymour Hoffman.

**What Rats Won't Do** (1998)
**Director:** Alastair Reid. **Writers:** Steve Coombes, William Osborne, Dave Robinson. **Producers:** Tim Bevan, Eric Fellner, Simon Wright. **Cast:** Natascha McElhone, James Frain, Charles Dance.

**Elizabeth** (1998)
**Director:** Shekhar Kapur. **Writer:** Michael Hirst.
**Producers:** Tim Bevan, Eric Fellner, Alison Owen.
**Co-Producers:** Liza Chasin, Debra Hayward.
**Cinematography:** Remi Adefarasin. **Production Design:** John Myhre. **Costume:** Alexandra Byrne.
**Hair and Make-up:** Jenny Shircore. **Music:** David Hirschfelder. **Cast:** Cate Blanchett, Geoffrey Rush, Joseph Fiennes, Christopher Eccleston, Sir Richard Attenborough, Vincent Cassel.

**The Hi-Lo Country** (1998)
**Director:** Stephen Frears. **Writer:** Walon Green (based on the book by Max Evans). **Producers:** Tim Bevan, Barbara De Fina, Eric Fellner, Martin Scorsese.
**Exec. Producer:** Rudd Simmons. **Co-Producer:** Liza Chasin. **Cinematography:** Oliver Stapleton.
**Music:** Carter Burwell. **Cast:** Woody Harrelson, Billy Crudup, Sam Elliott, Patricia Arquette, Penélope Cruz.

**Plunkett & Macleane** (1999)
**Director:** Jake Scott. **Writers:** Selwyn Roberts, Robert Wade, Neal Purvis, Charles McKeown.
**Producers:** Tim Bevan, Eric Fellner, Rupert Harvey.
**Co-Producers:** Jon Finn, Natascha Wharton.
**Cinematographer:** John Mathieson. **Costume:** Janty Yates. **Music:** Craig Armstrong. **Cast:** Jonny Lee Miller, Robert Carlyle, Ken Stott, Sir Michael Gambon, Liv Tyler.

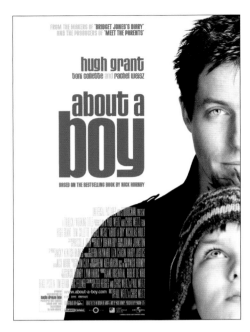

**Notting Hill** (1999)
**Director:** Roger Michell. **Writer:** Richard Curtis.
**Producer:** Duncan Kenworthy. **Exec. Producers:**
Tim Bevan, Eric Fellner, Richard Curtis.
**Cinematographer:** Michael Coulter. **Production
Design:** Stuart Craig. **Music:** Trevor Jones. **Cast:**
Julia Roberts, Hugh Grant, Rhys Ifans, Tim McInnerny,
Gina McKee, Emma Chambers, Hugh Bonneville.

**O Brother, Where Art Thou?** (2000)
**Director:** Joel Coen. **Writers:** Joel Coen and
Ethan Coen (based on Homer's **Odyssey**).
**Producer:** Ethan Coen. **Exec. Producers:** Tim
Bevan, Eric Fellner. **Cinematographer:** Roger
Deakins. **Editor:** Tricia Cooke, Roderick Jaynes.
**Production Design:** Dennis Gassner. **Music:** T-
Bone Burnett, Carter Burwell, Chris Thomas King.
**Cast:** George Clooney, John Turturro, Tim Blake-
Nelson, John Goodman, Holly Hunter.

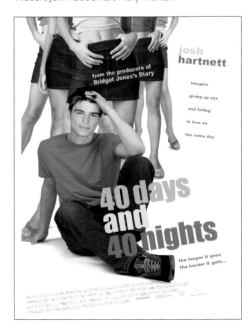

**Billy Elliot** (WT²) (2000)
**Director:** Stephen Daldry. **Writer:** Lee Hall.
**Producers:** Greg Brenman, Jon Finn. **Exec.
Producers:** Charles Brand, Tessa Ross, David M
Thompson, Natascha Wharton.
**Cinematographer:** Brian Tufano. **Music:** Stephen
Warbeck. **Cast:** Jamie Bell, Julie Walters.

**The Man Who Cried** (2000)
**Director:** Sally Potter. **Writer:** Sally Potter.
**Producer:** Christopher Sheppard. **Exec.
Producers:** Simona Benzakein, Tim Bevan, Eric
Fellner. **Cinematographer:** Sasha Vierny.
**Costume:** Lindy Hemming. **Cast:** Christina Ricci,
Cate Blanchett, John Turturro, Johnny Depp.

**High Fidelity** (2000) (for Touchstone Pictures)
**Director:** Stephen Frears. **Writers:** Steve Pink, D
V DeVincentis, John Cusack, Scott Rosenberg (based
on the book by Nick Hornby). **Producers:** Tim
Bevan, Rudd Simmons. **Exec. Producers:** Liza
Chasin, Alan Greenspan, Mike Newell.
**Co-Producers:** John Cusack, D V DeVincentis,
Steve Pink. **Cinematographer:** Seamus McGarvey.
**Editor:** Mick Audsley. **Music:** Howard Shore. **Cast:**
John Cusack, Iben Hjejle, Jack Black, Catherine Zeta-
Jones, Joan Cusack, Tim Robbins.

**Captain Corelli's Mandolin** (2001)
**Director:** John Madden. **Writer:** Shawn Slovo
(based on the book by Louis de Bernières).
**Producers:** Tim Bevan, Eric Fellner, Mark Huffam,
Kevin Loader. **Co-Producers:** Liza Chasin, Jane
Frazer, Debra Hayward. **Cinematography:** John
Toll. **Editor:** Mick Audsley. **Production Design:**
Jim Clay. **Music:** Stephen Warbeck. **Cast:** Nicolas
Cage, Penélope Cruz, John Hurt, Christian Bale.

**Bridget Jones's Diary** (2001)
**Director:** Sharon Maguire. **Writers:** Helen Fielding
(based on her own book) Andrew Davies, Richard
Curtis. **Producers:** Tim Bevan, Eric Fellner, Jonathan
Cavendish. **Co-Producers:** Liza Chasin, Debra
Hayward. **Exec. Producer:** Helen Fielding.
**Cast:** Renée Zellweger, Colin Firth, Hugh Grant.

**The Man Who Wasn't There** (2001)
**Director:** Joel Coen. **Writers:** Joel Coen and
Ethan Coen. **Producer:** Ethan Coen. **Co-
Producer:** John Cameron. **Exec. Producers:** Tim
Bevan, Eric Fellner. **Cinematographer:** Roger
Deakins. **Editor:** Roderick Jaynes, Tricia Cooke.
**Production Design:** Dennis Gassner. **Music:**
Carter Burwell. **Cast:** Billy Bob Thornton, Frances
McDormand, Michael Badalucco, James Gandolfini.

**Long Time Dead** (WT²) (2001)
**Director:** Marcus Adams. **Writers:** Eitan Arussi,
Chris Baker, Daniel Bronzite, Andy Day. **Producer:**
James Gay-Rees. **Exec. Producers:** Tim Bevan, Eric
Fellner, Jon Finn, Natascha Wharton. **Cast:** Joe
Absolom, Lara Belmont, Lukas Haas.

**My Little Eye** (WT²) (2002)
**Director:** Marc Evans. **Writers:** David Hilton,
James Watkins. **Producers:** Jon Finn, Alan
Greenspan, David Hilton, Jane Villiers,. **Exec.
Producers:** Tim Bevan, Eric Fellner, Natascha
Wharton. **Cast:** Sean Cw Johnson, Jennifer Sky.

**40 Days and 40 Nights** (2002)
**Director:** Michael Lehmann. **Writer:** Rob Perez.
**Producers:** Tim Bevan, Eric Fellner, Michael London.
**Exec. Producers:** Liza Chasin, Debra Hayward.
**Cast:** Josh Hartnett, Shannyn Sossamon.

**Ali G Indahouse** (WT²) (2002)
**Director:** Mark Mylod. **Writers:** Sacha Baron
Cohen, Dan Mazer. **Producers:** Tim Bevan, Eric
Fellner, Dan Mazer. **Exec. Producers:** Sacha Baron
Cohen, Peter Fincham, Natascha Wharton. **Cast:**
Sacha Baron Cohen, Sir Michael Gambon, Charles
Dance, Kellie Bright.

**About a Boy** (2002)
**Directors:** Chris Weitz, Paul Weitz . **Writers:**
Peter Hedges, Chris Weitz, Paul Weitz (based on
book by Nick Hornby). **Producers:** Tim Bevan,
Robert de Niro, Brad Epstein, Eric Fellner, Jane
Rosenthal. **Co-Producers:** Nicky Kentish Barnes,
Liza Chasin, Debra Hayward, Hardy Justice.
**Cinematography:** Remi Adefarasin. **Production
Design:** Jim Clay. **Music:** Damon Gough.
**Cast:** Hugh Grant, Toni Collette, Rachel Weisz,
Nicholas Hoult.

**The Guru** (2002)
**Director:** Daisy von Scherler Mayer. **Writer:**
Tracey Jackson. **Producers:** Tim Bevan, Eric Fellner,
Michael London. **Exec. Producers:** Liza Chasin,
Debra Hayward, Shekhar Kapur. **Cast:** Heather
Graham, Marisa Tomei, Jimi Mistry.

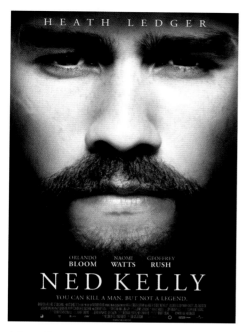

**Johnny English** (2003)
**Director**: Peter Howitt. **Writers:** Neal Purvis, Robert Wade, William Davies. **Producers:** Tim Bevan, Eric Fellner, Mark Huffam. **Co-Producers:** Jo Burn, Liza Chasin, Debra Hayward. **Cinematographer:** Remi Adefarasin. **Cast:** Rowan Atkinson, Natalie Imbruglia, John Malkovich.

**Ned Kelly** (2003)
**Director:** Gregor Jordan. **Writer:** John M McDonagh (based on book by Robert Drewe). **Producers:** Lynda House, Nelson Woss. **Exec. Producers:** Tim Bevan, Eric Fellner, Tim White. **Co-Producers:** Liza Chasin, Debra Hayward. **Cinematographer:** Oliver Stapleton. **Cast:** Heath Ledger, Orlando Bloom, Geoffrey Rush, Naomi Watts, Laurence Kinlan, Philip Barantini, Rachel Griffiths.

**Love Actually** (2003)
**Director:** Richard Curtis. **Writer:** Richard Curtis. **Producers:** Duncan Kenworthy, Tim Bevan, Eric Fellner. **Cinematographer:** Michael Coulter. **Production Design:** Jim Clay. **Costume:** Joanna Johnston. **Music:** Craig Armstrong. **Cast:** Laura Linney, Liam Neeson, Martine McCutcheon, Rowan Atkinson, Chiewtel Ejiofor, Colin Firth, Hugh Grant, Keira Knightley, Andrew Lincoln, Lucia Moniz, Bill Nighy, Alan Rickman, Emma Thompson, Billy Bob Thornton.

**Calcium Kid** (WT²) (2003)
**Director:** Alex De Rakoff. **Writer:** Derek Boyle, Alex De Rakoff, Raymond Friel. **Producer:** Natascha Wharton. **Executive Producers:** Tim Bevan, Eric Fellner, **Cast:** Orlando Bloom.

**Thirteen** (2003)
**Director:** Catherine Hardwicke. **Producers:** Jeffrey Levy-Hinte, Michael London. **Executive Producers:** Tim Bevan, Eric Fellner, Liza Chasin, Holly Hunter **Writers:** Catherine Hardwicke, Nikki Reed. **Cast:** Holly Hunter and Evan Rachel Wood.

**The Shape Of Things** (2003)
**Director:** Neil Labute. **Writer:** Neil LaBute **Executive Producers:** Tim Bevan & Eric Fellner **Producers:** Neil LaBute, Gail Mutrux, Philip Steuer, Rachel Weisz **Cast:** Gretchen Mol, Paul Rudd,Rachel Weisz, Frederick Weller.

**Gettin' Square** (2003)
**Director:** Jonathan Teplitzky. **Writer:** Chris Nyst. **Executive Producers:** Tim Bevan, Eric Fellner, Michael Gudinski, Kris Noble. **Producer:** Tim White, Trish Lake, Martin Fabinyi. **Cast:** Tim Spall, Sam Worthington, David Wenham.

**Shaun of The Dead** (WT²) (2004)
**Director:** Edgar Wright. **Writers:** Edgar Wright, Simon Pegg. **Producer:** Nira Park. **Exec Producers:** Tim Bevan, Eric Fellner, Natascha Wharton, Alison Owen, Jim Wilson **Cast:** Simon Pegg, Nick Frost, Kate Ashfield, Jessica Stevenson, Bill Nighy, Penelope Wilton, Rafe Spall.

**Wimbledon** (2004)
**Director:** Richard Loncraine. **Writers:** Jennifer Flackett, Mark Levin and Adam Brooks **Producers:** Tim Bevan, Eric Fellner, Mary Richards and David Livingstone. **Co-producers:** Liza Chasin, Debra Hayward. **Cast:** Paul Bettany, Kirsten Dunst.

**Thunderbirds** (2004)
**Director:** Jonathan Frakes. **Writers:** Michael McCullers, William Osborne. **Producers:** Tim Bevan, Eric Fellner, Mark Huffam. **Co-producers:** Jo Burn, Debra Hayward, Liza Chasin. **Cinematographer** : Brendan Galvin. **Production Design:** John Beard. **Cast:** Bill Paxton, Ben Kingsley, Anthony Edwards, Sophia Myles, Ron Cook.

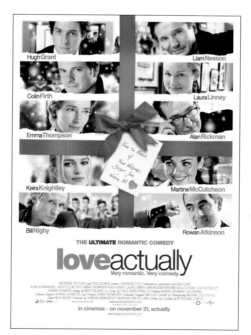

# FILMS PRODUCED BY ERIC FELLNER AT INITIAL FILMS:

**Sid and Nancy** (1986)
**Director:** Alex Cox. **Writers:** Alex Cox, Abbe Wool. **Producer:** Eric Fellner. **Exec. Producer:** Margaret Matheson. **Cinematographer:** Roger Deakins. **Cast:** Gary Oldman, Chloe Webb.

**Straight To Hell** (1987)
**Director**: Alex Cox. **Writer:** Alex Cox, Dick Rude. **Producer:** Eric Fellner. **Production Design:** Andrew McAlpine. **Cast:** Dick Rude, Courtney Love, Joe Strummer.

**Pascali's Island** (1988)
**Director:** James Dearden. **Writer:** James Dearden (based on book by Barry Unsworth). **Producers:** Tania Windsor Blunden, Paul Raphael, Mirella Sklavounou. **Exec. Producer:** Eric Fellner **Cinematography**: Roger Deakins. **Cast:** Ben Kingsley, Charles Dance, Helen Mirren.

**The Rachel Papers** (1989)
**Director:** Damian Harris. **Writer:** Damian Harris (based on book by Martin Amis). **Producer:** Andrew S. Karsch. **Exec. Producers:** Eric Fellner, James T. Roe III. **Co-Producer:** Paul Raphael **Cast:** Dexter Fletcher, Ione Skye, Jonathan Pryce, James Spader, Michael Gambon.

**Hidden Agenda** (1990)
**Director:** Ken Loach. **Writer:** Jim Allen. **Producer:** Eric Fellner. **Co-Producer:** Rebecca O'Brien. **Cinematographer**: Clive Tickner. **Music**: Stewart Copeland. **Cast:** Frances McDormand, Brian Cox, Brad Dourif.

**A Kiss Before Dying** (1991)
**Director:** James Dearden. **Writer:** James Dearden (based on book by Ira Levin). **Producer:** Robert Lawrence. **Exec. Producer:** Eric Fellner. **Cinematographer:** Mike Southon. **Production Design:** Jim Clay. **Music:** Howard Shore. **Cast**: Sean Young, Matt Dillon, Max von Sydow.

**Liebestraum** (1992)
**Director:** Mike Figgis. **Writer:** Mike Figgis. **Producer:** Eric Fellner. **Cast:** Bill Pullman, Kim Novak.

**Wild West** (1992)
**Director:** David Attwood. **Writer**: Harwant Bains. **Producer:** Eric Fellner. **Co-Producer:** Nicky Kentish Barnes. **Cast:** Naveen Andrews, Sarita Choudhury.

## CHAPTER OPENER CAPTIONS

*p2* **'Is it raining? I hadn't noticed':
Carrie (Andie MacDowell) and
Charles (Hugh Grant) kiss in
the final scene of** *Four Weddings
and A Funeral; p6* **'Genuinely Tiny
Knickers':** *Bridget Jones's Diary;
p20:* **Johnny (Daniel Day-Lewis,
left) and Omar (Gordon
Warnecke) proudly stand outside
their Beautiful Laundrette;** *p62:*
**Rebels with a Cause: Nancy
Spungen (Chloe Webb) and Sid
Vicious (Gary Oldman) in** *Sid
and Nancy; p74:* **Cate Blanchett
as the Virgin Queen in** *Elizabeth;
p174:* **Billy Elliot (Jamie Bell)
dances in his bedroom**

## KISSES PAGES CAPTIONS

*p8-9 Top Row, Left to right:* **Carrie
(Andie MacDowell) and Charles
(Hugh Grant) –** *Four Weddings
and a Funeral;* **Kate Lemmon
(Emma Thompson) and Dexter
King (Jeff Goldblum –** *The Tall
Guy;* **Johnny (Daniel Day Lewis)
and Omar (Gordon Warnecke)
–** *My Beautiful Laundrette;*
**Albertine (Anne Parillaud) and
Avik (Jason Scott Lee) –** *Map of
the Human Heart; 2nd Row, Left to
right:* **Ali G (Sacha Baron Cohen)
and Me Julie (Kellie Bright) –** *Ali
G Indahouse;* **Sheri (Juliette
Lewis) and Jack Grimaldi (Gary
Oldman) –** *Romeo is Bleeding;*
**Sharonna (Heather Graham)
and Ramu Gupta (Jimi Mistry)
–** *The Guru;* **Josepha O'Neil
(Penélope Cruz) and Pete
Calder (Billy Crudup) –** *The
Hi-Lo Country; 3rd Row, Left to right:*
**Ellen/Dorothy Carlsson (Sean
Young) and Jonathan Corliss
(Matt Dillon) –** *A Kiss Before
Dying;* **Pelagia (Penélope Cruz)
and Captain Corelli (Nicolas
Cage) –** *Captain Corelli's
Mandolin;* **Isabella (Tilda
Swinton) and Edward II (Steven
Waddington) –** *Edward II;* **The
Painter (Jon Bon Jovi) and
Rebecca Trager Lott (Elizabeth
Perkins) –** *Moonlight and
Valentino; 4th Row, L to R:* **Bridget
Jones (Renée Zellweger) and
Mark Darcy (Colin Firth) –**
*Bridget Jones's Diary;* **Ned Kelly
(Heath Ledger) and Julia Cook
(Naomi Watts) –** *Ned Kelly;*
**William Thacker (Hugh Grant)
and Anna Scott (Julia Roberts)
–** *Notting Hill;* **Peter (Chiwetel
Ejiofor) and Juliet (Keira
Knightley) –** *Love Actually*

## PHOTOGRAPHY CREDITS

*p.1 Left to right:* Mike Laye © 1985
Working Title Films Ltd. All Rights
Reserved; Alex Bailey © 1998
Universal City Studios, Inc. All Rights
Reserved. Courtesy of Universal
Studios Licensing LLLP; Merrick
Morton © 1998 PolyGram Filmed
Entertainment, Inc. All Rights Reserved.
Courtesy of Universal Studios
Licensing LLLP; Paul Chedlow
© 2001 Universal Studios/Studio
Canal/Miramax Film Corporation. All
Rights Reserved. Courtesy of Universal
Studios Licensing LLLP; *p2* Stephen
Morley © 1994 Orion Pictures
Corporation. All Rights Reserved.
Courtesy of MGM Clip+Still; *p6*
Alex Bailey © 2001 Universal
Studios/Studio Canal/Miramax Film
Corporation. All Rights Reserved.
Courtesy of Universal Studios
Licensing LLLP; *p8-9 First line, left to
right,:* Stephen Morley © 1994 Orion
Pictures Corporation. All Rights
Reserved. Courtesy of MGM
Clip+Still; Ian Pleeth © 1989 London
Weekend Television, Ltd. All Rights
Reserved. Courtesy of MGM
Clip+Still; Mike Laye © 1985 Working
Title Films Ltd. All Rights Reserved;
Kirk Tougas © 1992 Universal City
Studios, Inc. All Rights Reserved.
Courtesy of Universal Studios
Licensing LLLP; *Second line, left to right:*
Giles Keyte © 2002 Kalima
Productions GmbH & Co. KG. All
Rights Reserved. Courtesy of Universal
Studios Licensing LLLP; Demmie Todd
© 1994 Orion Pictures Corporation.
All Rights Reserved. Courtesy of
MGM Clip+Still; Catherine Matinson
© 2002 Universal Studios. All Rights
Reserved. Courtesy of Universal
Studios Licensing LLLP; Sidney Baldwin
© 1998 Universal Studios. All Rights
Reserved. Courtesy of Universal
Studios Licensing LLLP; *Third line left to
right:* David Appleby © 1991 Universal
Studios. All Rights Reserved. Courtesy
of Universal Studios Licensing LLLP;
Peter Mountain © 2001Universal
Studios /Studio Canal/Miramax Film
Corporation. All Rights Reserved.
Courtesy of Universal Studios
Licensing LLLP; Mike Laye © 1991
BBC Films. All Rights Reserved.
Courtesy of BBC Photo Library;
Shane Harvey © 1995 Orion Pictures
Corporation. All Rights Reserved.
Courtesy of MGM Clip+Still; *Fourth
line left to right:* Alex Bailey © 2001
Universal Studios/Studio
Canal/Miramax Film Corporation. All
Rights Reserved. Courtesy of Universal
Studios Licensing LLLP; Carolyn Johns
© 2003 WT Venture LLC. All Rights

Reserved. Courtesy of Universal
Studios Licensing LLLP; Clive Coote
© 1999 Universal City Studios, Inc. All
Rights Reserved. Courtesy of Universal
Studios Licensing LLLP; Peter Mountain
© 2003 WT Venture LLC. All Rights
Reserved. Courtesy of Universal
Studios Licensing LLLP; *p10* Gaby
Dellal © Gaby Dellal; *p12 Left:* Mike
Laye © 1985 Working Title Films Ltd.
All Rights Reserved; *Right:* Alex Bailey
©1998 Universal City Studios, Inc. All
Rights Reserved. Courtesy of Universal
Studios Licensing LLLP; *p13 Left:* Mike
Laye © 1986 Working Title Films Ltd.
All Rights Reserved; *Right:* Peter
Mountain © 2001 Universal
Studios/Studio Canal/Miramax Film
Corporation. All Rights Reserved.
Courtesy of Universal Studios
Licensing LLLP; *p14* Bertrand Rindoff
© Bertrand Rindoff/Alpha Press; *p17*
Alex Bailey © 1998 Universal City
Studios, Inc. All Rights Reserved.
Courtesy of Universal Studios
Licensing LLLP; *p19* Peter Mountain
© Peter Mountain/Katz Pictures; *p20*
© 1985 Working Title Films Ltd. All
Rights Reserved; *p22 Above:* David
Appleby © 1988 Working Title Films
Ltd. All Rights Reserved; *Below:* Mike
Laye © 1986 British Film Institute. All
Rights Reserved; *p23* David Appleby
© 1988 Working Title Films Ltd. All
Rights Reserved; *p25* Anton Corbijn
© Anton Corbijn; *p26* Mike Laye
© 1985 Working Title Films Ltd. All
Rights Reserved; *p27 Above:* Simon
Mein © 1986 Zenith Productions. All
Rights Reserved; *Below:* Mike Laye
© 1986 Working Title Films Ltd. All
Rights Reserved; *p28-29, 31, 32, 34,
37, 39* Mike Laye © 1985 Working
Title Films Ltd. All Rights Reserved;
*p40-41, 43, 44, 45* Ian Pleeth ©
Channel Four Television Corporation
1987. All Rights Reserved. Licensed by
4 Ventures Ltd; *p46, 47* Mike Laye ©
1986 Working Title Films Ltd. All Rights
Reserved; *p48, 49, 51* Mike Laye ©
1987 Working Title Films Ltd. All Rights
Reserved; *p52, 53, 54, 55, 57* David
Appleby © 1988 Working Title Films
Ltd. All Rights Reserved; *p58 Above:*
© 1989 London Weekend Television,
Ltd. All Rights Reserved. Courtesy of
MGM Clip+Still; *p58 Below, 59, 60, 61*
Ian Pleeth © 1989 London Weekend
Television, Ltd. All Rights Reserved.
Courtesy of MGM Clip+Still; *p62, 65,
66-67* Simon Mein © 1986 Zenith
Productions. All Rights Reserved; *p68,
69* Tom Collins © 1988 Avenue
Entertainment, Inc. All Rights Reserved.
Courtesy of MGM Clip+Still; *p70*
David Appleby © 1990 Orion Pictures
Corporation. All Rights Reserved.
Courtesy of MGM Clip+Still; *p72, 73*

David Appleby © 1991 Universal
Studios. All Rights Reserved. Courtesy
of Universal Studios Licensing LLLP;
*p74* Alex Bailey © 1998 Universal
City Studios, Inc. All Rights Reserved.
Courtesy of Universal Studios
Licensing LLLP; *p76, 77* Mike Laye
© 1991 BBC Films. All Rights
Reserved. Courtesy of BBC Photo
Library; *p78, 79, 80, 82-83* Takashi
Seida © 1992 Universal City Studios,
Inc. All Rights Reserved. Courtesy of
Universal Studios Licensing LLLP; *p81,
85* Kirk Tougas © 1992 Universal City
Studios, Inc. All Rights Reserved.
Courtesy of Universal Studios
Licensing LLLP; *p86 Above:* Sam J. Jones
© 1992 PolyGram Holdings. All Rights
Reserved. Courtesy of Universal
Studios Licensing LLLP; *Below left:*
© 1997 PolyGram Filmed
Entertainment, Inc. All Rights Reserved.
Courtesy of Universal Studios
Licensing LLLP; *Below right:* © 1997
Working Title Films Ltd. All Rights
Reserved. Courtesy of Universal
Studios Licensing LLLP; *p87 Above:*
Nick Wall © Nick Wall; *Below left:* ©
1996 Orion Pictures Corporation. All
Rights Reserved. Courtesy of MGM
Clip+Still; *Below right:* © 1998
Universal City Studios, Inc. All Rights
Reserved. Courtesy of Universal
Studios Licensing LLLP;
*p88-89, 91, 94, 96* Stephen Morley
© 1994 Orion Pictures Corporation.
All Rights Reserved. Courtesy of
MGM Clip+Still; *p93* © 1994 Orion
Pictures Corporation. All Rights
Reserved. Courtesy of MGM
Clip+Still; *p98-99* © 1994 Orion
Pictures Corporation. All Rights
Reserved. Courtesy of MGM
Clip+Still; *p100* © 1994 Orion
Pictures Corporation. All Rights
Reserved. Courtesy of MGM
Clip+Still; *p102-103, 104, 105* Jim
Bridges © 1994 Warner Bros. All
Rights Reserved. Courtesy of Universal
Studios Licensing LLLP; *p106-107*
Albert Watson © Albert Watson;
*p108* John Harwood © 1993 Orion
Pictures Corporation. All Rights
Reserved. Courtesy of MGM
Clip+Still; *p109* Robert Zuckerman
© 1995 Orion Pictures Corporation.
All Rights Reserved. Courtesy of
MGM Clip+Still; *p110* Demmie Todd
© 1994 Orion Pictures Corporation.
All Rights Reserved. Courtesy of
MGM Clip+Still; *p111* Shane Harvey
© 1995 Orion Pictures Corporation.
All Rights Reserved. Courtesy of
MGM Clip+Still; *p112* Etienne George
© 1995 Orion Pictures Corporation.
All Rights Reserved. Courtesy of
MGM Clip+Still; *p114-115* Pamela
Hanson © Pamela Hanson; *p116, 117*

## FILMOGRAPHY POSTERS

## PRODUCTION ARTWORK